The Triangle Effect

YOUR INCREDIBLE JOURNEY TO POWER, BALANCE AND ENERGY

STEVEN T. FOLGATE

ARCHWAY
PUBLISHING

This book is a work of non-fiction. Unless otherwise noted, the author and the publisher make no explicit guarantees as to the accuracy of the information contained in this book, and in some cases, names of people and places have been altered to protect their privacy.

Archway Publishing books may be ordered through booksellers or by contacting:

Archway Publishing
1663 Liberty Drive
Bloomington, IN 47403
www.archwaypublishing.com
844-669-3957

Because of the dynamic nature of the Internet, any web addresses or links contained in this book may have changed since publication and may no longer be valid. The views expressed in this work are solely those of the author and do not necessarily reflect the views of the publisher, and the publisher hereby disclaims any responsibility for them.

ISBN: 978-1-6657-5013-4 (sc)
ISBN: 978-1-6657-5014-1 (e)

Library of Congress Control Number: 2023917476

Print information available on the last page.

Archway Publishing rev. date: 11/28/2023

DEDICATION

This book is dedicated to Denise, my wife of 40-plus years, who has stuck with me through good times and some "character building" times. When we met, I thought marriage was about finding the right person, and I certainly won the lottery in that area. Only later did I come to realize that marriage isn't so much about *finding* the right person—it's about *being* the right person. I'm so grateful that I met Denise at a very young age. It has been a miraculous journey, and I remain excited about experiencing the joy of life together in the future.

I also dedicate this book to my two precious daughters, Meghan Rochelle and Erin Nicole, who have taught me so much about life and the blessings of God. I'm grateful they married well because it's a joy to have Mike and Brock in our family.

Finally, the book is dedicated to the true joy in my life—our four grandchildren, McKenna Palmer, Clark Brady, Maxton Edward and Hogan William. Grandchildren are the greatest invention in the universe. I understand life in an amazing new way because of them. They inspired this book.

Love you all,

Steve

TABLE OF CONTENTS

INTRODUCTION

Part I | *Welcome to The Triangle Effect*

A black dog stands in the middle of an intersection in a town painted black. None of the street lights are working due to a power outage. A car with two broken headlights drives toward the dog but turns just in time to avoid hitting him. How could the driver have seen the dog in time?

Luckily for the dog, it was daylight—but you had to shift your perspective and abandon your assumptions to grasp that.

This little puzzle implies that the *angle* we view things from has a powerful effect on our perceptions and thus our understandings. That angle is the lens through which we see the world— and it determines how we view ourselves, other people and everything else in the universe around us.

This book explores and applies the profound concept that three different angles—inherent in that simple geometric shape, the triangle—are much more powerful than the single angle that many people use when they view the world.

I call this the Triangle Effect.

It flows from the idea that a single angle is limiting. But if we employ the Triangle Effect in our day-to-day lives, we open ourselves up to new perspectives, new ideas, new strategies— new ways of thinking and living and being.

As you'll see, that's what this book is all about. But first—a few words about how this book originated.

Part II | *A bookman and his index cards*

It's early morning, May, 1977, Smithville, Tennessee. The alarm clock sounds, and I roll out of bed at 5:30. Why is the alarm ringing at this unearthly time? For one thing, I want to take my customary 20-minute jog. But I also have to report for work within an hour and 15 minutes.

And it's a brutal work schedule for a group of us college students who are trying to earn fall tuition money:

- 6:00—Cold shower
- 6:15—Inspirational reading
- 6:45—Leave for the restaurant
- 7:00—Breakfast with the team
- 7:30—Do the Southwestern Company bookman song and dance in front of the restaurant. "It's a great day to be a bookman, and to be of good cheer," we sing.
- 7:35—Hit the streets and sell some product

The job requires us to knock on our first door before 8 a.m. and keep going strong until 9:30 p.m., six days a week. That's the schedule. Anything less, and management wouldn't be pleased.

So my summer job, after my freshman year of college, was to trudge from door to door selling Bibles and children's books.

We began the summer with a weeklong sales school, and then we were dispatched to our respective territories to work 80 hours a week for the next 12 weeks. (The company had calculated that we wouldn't make enough money to pay for our tuition if we didn't work the full 80 hours.)

Each workday was divided into three 4½-hour periods:

- 8–12:30
- 12:30–5
- 5–9:30 (the "gravy shift")

We were to give at least 10 product demonstrations during each period. Our motto: "Thirty demos a day keeps the negatives away."

This three-part schedule was my first experience with the "power of three"—which, of course, is exactly the focus of this book. Science proves that when we chunk bits of information into groups of three, they become more manageable, meaningful and easy to remember. A 13½- hour workday seemed much less overwhelming when it was split into three manageable units.

Nevertheless, the Southwestern job provided structure and a sense of future possibilities for me—a young man who until then had been more interested in partying than working. I got caught up in the rah-rah culture of sales, and I started believing that I could be successful if I'd buy into the idea of "controlling the controllables" and then let the rest take care of itself.

After all, who was I, just another kid in college, to question the philosophy and practices of a successful company that had been around for more than 110 years?

I knew nothing about sales—and even less about the Bible I was selling. As a kid, I appreciated the Bible only as a safe place to hide the cash my grandmothers gave me when my birthday and Christmas rolled around—because I knew no one in my family would ever open it.

But the Southwestern Company system worked for me. At the end of the summer, I had earned a big paycheck and was heading back to college. Compared to most of my friends back in Indiana, I had a lot more cash on hand because I worked 80 hours a week and didn't have any free time in which to spend my earnings.

More importantly, though, I had developed a sense of personal accomplishment and confidence. I was a different person by the end of that sales experience, and it felt great. A paradigm shift had taken place in my life. My beliefs about my life and my future had undergone a transformation during the three months of that summer.

The structure, the commitment, the inspirational books and slogans, the goal-setting processes, the new habits of productivity— they all made me feel called, pushed and energized. What happened that summer became an indelible part of me.

After my summer with Southwestern, I went back to college and changed my major to marketing. I also continued the early-morning habit I had acquired of reading inspirational material—but then I thought, *Why stop at 15 minutes?* I began to get up earlier and read for a full hour. I found rags-to-riches stories and positive-thinking books inspiring. And I learned that time spent reading made me much more productive in whatever I gave my time, energy and attention to.

Throughout the decades that followed my college years, I continued to read voraciously. I also developed the habit of jotting down, on 3x5 index cards, quotations and other material that I wanted to remember and perhaps share. All these years later, my thousands of cards fill a plastic tub.

Over time, writing those notes helped me realize that there were things in my life that made me less productive, less effective and more likely to fail—things like anxiety, fear, uncertainty, insecurity, selfishness, jealousy and ingratitude. (Some of these things seemed to come naturally to me, I'm afraid!)

But in contrast, I also became aware of traits that made me more productive, more effective and more in harmony with others. They included effort, discipline, courage, empathy, depth, sincerity, faith, thankfulness and selflessness. I needed to work hard at developing these traits, but the notes and cards helped keep me on track.

When I reviewed my thousands of note cards after a recent birthday, I realized that I had spent 40 years accumulating a treasure trove of information and even wisdom. I recognized that this collection of notes was one of my greatest assets, and I felt that it almost was begging to be shared. Also, I have found the 3x5 index card to be like a Swiss Army knife: simple, affordable and powerfully effective for us humans in this game of life.

That's when I began to think about writing a book as a means of organizing the index-card chaos. I even imagined that the tidbits I had collected could be a life-giving resource for readers—including, perhaps, my grandchildren one day.

Thus, the book you hold in your hands (or perhaps view on your device reader) is my attempt to consolidate and share some of the greatest hits from my "plastic tub of wisdom."

Part III | *Power, Balance, Energy*

Over the years, I've read dozens of books about business and personal productivity, and I'm certainly not knocking those books. They've done me a wealth of good, and I suppose that I do tend to see the world through a "productivity lens."

However, I hope that *The Triangle Effect* offers more than merely a blueprint for being more productive and successful— although I do hope that's one byproduct! More broadly, I trust that the book will illuminate the path for readers to become *better and happier people* through a paradigm-shift process— and it's one that's really going to happen if you punch its ticket.

We all want to live freely, be authentic and develop into the best-possible version of ourselves. We aspire to feel as if we're truly alive—not as if life were simply happening to us. When our goal is to *be*, then living as though we're 100% alive isn't just a pipe dream—it becomes an attainable reality.

I have a quote from George Bernard Shaw in my precious index-card collection that illustrates this point: "This is the true joy in life: Being used for a purpose recognized by yourself as a mighty one, being a force of nature instead of a feverish, selfish little clod of ailments and grievances, complaining that the world will not devote itself to making you happy. I am of the opinion that my life belongs to the whole community, and as long as I live, it is my privilege to do for it what I can. I want to be thoroughly used up when I die. For the harder I work, the more I live. I rejoice in life for its own sake. Life is no brief candle to me. It is a sort of splendid torch which I have got hold of for the moment, and I want to make it burn as brightly as possible before handing it on to future generations."

I believe that the Triangle Effect draws us closer to this "fully alive state" in several ways. First, it teaches us to truly connect with the world around us. When we're consciously immersed in our surroundings, aware of how the world is moving around us, then we're also tuning in to ourselves. Knowing the truth sets us free, so in order to have absolute freedom, we need absolute truth—and that involves awareness.

The Triangle Effect, as we've already seen, also equips us with a holistic approach to *power*, *balance* and *energy*—three of the central concepts of this book. These concepts aren't items to check off on a to-do list, and we don't experience them by working harder and faster than everyone else. Instead, they make us better from the inside out—they're about helping us to see our value and our purpose.

Finally, the Triangle Effect is dependent on our *actions*. All our words mean nothing if we aren't willing to make new goals and then chase them down with deliberate planning, baby steps and leaps of faith. Our paradigm will shift only if we take steps in a different direction.

Naturally, all triangles have three angles, and that's a concept I use throughout the book when I refer to the "power of three."

You'll note that this introduction is divided into three parts. And if you consult the table of contents, you'll see that the book also has three major parts—Power, Balance and Energy. And then, true to form, each of these sections has three chapters.

Power, Balance and Energy are the organizing principles of our enterprise—the overarching, crucially important things we need to understand and embrace if we're to achieve the kind of success that we're striving for.

The first part of the book, Power, explores how *grit, gratitude* and *goals* can help us rearrange our mental furniture and enable us to achieve more of the things that we truly value.

The second part probes three aspects of Balance—*physical, mental* and *financial*—that have tremendous impact on our well-being.

And the third and final part, Energy, takes us on a journey *inward, outward* and *upward* as we learn how to fulfill our mission in life.

My hope is that this book's focus on the life-altering possibilities of power, balance and energy will strike you in such a way that you simply *must* move toward incorporating their insights and principles into your daily life. We're working toward pursuing growth and living our best life—one infused with freedom, power and peace.

When you finish reading *The Triangle Effect*, I hope that the pages will be dog-eared, heavily highlighted and inked with exclamations of personal insight. Ultimately, I hope you'll be transformed, overwhelmed and inspired by the new understandings that flow from using the *power of three* for more power, balance and energy in your life.

—*Steve Folgate*

PART I

---※◆◈◆※---

POWER

As we embark on an exploration of Power in the next three chapters—entitled Grit, Gratitude and Goals—we think for a moment about how we'd all like to have more power. Human nature nudges us to seek a little more power from time to time.

Of course, I'm not talking about the kind of "superhero power" that gives us the ability to leap tall buildings in a single bound. Nor am I talking about political power or the kind of brute force that can bend people to our will.

Instead, I'm talking about the kind of power we need in order to have an extraordinary, magnificent and abundant life.

Imagine that you're passing a semi-truck on the interstate and you see in the rear-view mirror that you have a pack of impatient drivers on your tail. Maybe someone is honking or flashing headlights at you. No one likes to be in this position. But one of the things I love about driving a high-performance car is that I can slam the pedal to the metal—feel the rush of a little g-force for a second!—and zip right by the truck and out of a tense situation. It's that simple when we have sufficient power under the hood.

I've employed a driving analogy here, but imagine how great it would be if we could harness that kind of power in our personal lives. Well, we can. That's what the Power section of this book is about. I call it the power of "three Gs"—Grit, Gratitude and Goals.

CHAPTER ONE

GRIT

"The brick walls are there to stop the
people who don't want it badly enough.
They're there to stop the other people."
—*Randy Pausch*

One of my earliest childhood memories is burned into my mind because it was such an emotional experience. I couldn't have been much more than 4½ years old when my mom joined a bowling league. After my older sister and brother were in school, my mother felt it might be a good idea for her to have some fun with her friends and for me to get out into the broader world at the same time.

So, Mom dropped me off in the childcare room that the bowling alley had set up for the mothers in the league. However, when I was introduced to this new plan that my mom had in mind, it was a shock to my system. I decided that I didn't want any part of this scheme— *not on your life*. I had never been away from my mom in this kind of scary situation, and I wasn't about to let this be the first time. "I want my mom!" I wailed at the top of my lungs. *"I want my mom!"*

"She's not coming back for a while, buddy," one of the daycare workers told me. I was advised to play with the other children.

Nope. I was adamant. I was either going to get my mom back or...well, there was no other option. I carried on with my tantrum until the staff moved me into a separate, soundproof room. There, my plight got even worse. I looked through the window at the other kids, and they laughed at my beet-red face as I screamed and pounded on the walls.

"I want my mommy!" I hollered, and I cried and screamed some more. Then I decided to switch tactics: I held my breath and stared at the staff with defiance. I must have been in danger of passing out, because they finally capitulated and returned me to my embarrassed mother.

That was my first memory of what I'm calling *grit*. Grit is a combination of passion for what we want and perseverance in seeking a long-term, meaningful goal. In that bowling alley, a scared and distraught little Steve learned what it meant to fight until he got what he wanted.

Perhaps my experience as a youngster isn't a great example of what we're talking about in this chapter—or perhaps it is. But if nothing else, this story comes to my mind when I think about what it means to have grit.

If little Steve could muster enough determination to get the job done, then so can I as an adult. And so can you.

What does grit actually mean?

What is grit? Simply put, it's a character trait that's reflected in the way we tirelessly chase after our goals—especially if it takes a while to achieve them. Actually, it's even more than that. Grit is also about having a deep passion for those goals in the relentless pursuit of attaining them.

A gritty person is less likely to give up when they hit a brick wall. They're less likely to quit the team in the middle of the season.

They're more likely to pursue that challenging goal all the way to the end, regardless of the setbacks or trials they encounter along the way.

Psychologist and author Angela Duckworth has done some interesting work in this area. Her research shows a strong correlation between grit and the success that some students have in school. Regardless of their natural intelligence, students who worked harder and longer proved to be more successful in the long term than those who were smarter but less gritty.

Some have challenged Duckworth's research, claiming that she sees "grit" where she's really measuring other variables such as IQ and social location. It's true that the science on grit is fairly young, with only a few long-term studies having been conducted thus far. It's probably an open question what social science eventually will say about grit.

I'm not an academic researcher (or a gambler), so I won't place a wager on what Duckworth's line of research eventually will reveal about the role of grit in our lives. However, I can say that as I pursued success and strove to reach my life goals, grit has played a prominent role.

Grit on the links

Let me share an insight about grit that I acquired through my lifelong love affair with the game of golf. But the lesson applies to whatever it is that someone is passionate about.

One day early in my insurance career, I made my typical after-lunch stop at the local golf course to practice on the putting green for about 20 minutes. But on this particular occasion, I spotted someone I recognized but didn't know personally. I'll call him "The Coach."

He was a legend in local golfing circles, and I knew from reading the sports pages that he had won pretty much every golf tournament in the region. At the city, county and state levels, he'd collected multiple victories. He was short, stocky and a mass of solid muscle—the personification of "power and grit."

There he was, 20 feet from me on the practice putting green. I knew all about him, but I had no reason to think he knew—or cared—who I was. He was into some kind of intense practice trance that I knew I shouldn't interrupt. I tried to focus on my practice and stay out of his way, but I couldn't help watching him do his work. The passion, the concentration, the intensity—it was inspiring and intoxicating.

Finally, I just couldn't take it anymore, and my bold, brash salesman nature got the best of me. I walked over and introduced myself, saying that I knew who he was and that it was an honor to shake his hand. I asked if he'd be willing to share the secret of his low scores, and I proudly explained that sometimes I practiced my putting for up to a half hour.

I'll never forget what he told me. I certainly wouldn't say that he snarled at me—he was a classy guy—but he looked at me with a degree of intensity. He said, *"You call that practice?"*

He went on to relate how many *hours* he spent on the putting green in a single practice session.

I sheepishly thanked him and walked away, wondering if it was humanly possible to practice that much. I knew that after I practiced 40 minutes, my back would be killing me. But I thought that maybe if I built up my strength and endurance, I could improve my game. With my new passion and goal, I went to work.

Day after day, I kept coming back to the practice green and working a little longer. Weeks and months went by. I climbed from 45 minutes to 60 and eventually to 90-minute practice sessions. The hardest part was staying mentally focused for that long. (Later in life, I learned that was the secret.) I set up various mind games to help me keep my concentration sharp.

I'm happy to say that all the hard work paid off. A year and a half later, I went out to play a round with a friend. He paused after

15 holes and said, "Hey, do you know that you're two under par?" I had never shot a round in the 60s, and this course was a par 70, so I had a real chance. I drew on the resources of all that practice and finished with a 68.

I went on to play in local tournaments over the next 25 years, and I'm sure about this one thing: I wouldn't have been able to achieve that level of play or have those decades of enjoyment without the lesson I learned about "golf grit" from a dedicated player all those years before.

Strength in the moment

Whatever our interests, we can generate more power in our lives with grit. But the funny thing is that as I look back on the various chapters of my life, I never really recognized that I was drawing on the resources of grit in the midst of tough circumstances. Instead, hindsight helps me understand how that factor illuminated the paths that led me to where I am today in business and in life.

I'm not afraid to be honest and say that I haven't displayed grit every time I've run into the proverbial brick wall. I wish I could have some of those days and decisions back. I like to think that I'd put on my "grit gear" and power on through.

But I do clearly recall a host of times when grit came to the rescue during some challenges that involved various business mergers and acquisitions. Nobody would have blamed me for throwing in the towel in those tough spots. In fact, sometimes commercial loan officers as well as my friends and relatives encouraged me to ditch my plans and dreams, arguing that there were safer ways to build a business and provide for my family's future.

But now I understand that life isn't about seeking safe harbors. That's why we need grit to give us strength in the moment and courage in the midst of adversity. As John A. Shedd noted in his 1928 book *Salt from My Attic*: "A ship is safe in harbor, but that's not what ships are built for."

Developing grit

How do we develop this quality? Well, like many things in life, it must be practiced. Perhaps the executive summary of the instruction manual for grit could consist of two words: *Don't quit.*

I've always been a big fan of motivational phrases, and you can bet that my tub of 3x5 cards contains more than a few. But some of these phrases are basically part of the cultural air that we breathe— everybody knows them. It's likely that any reader of this book would have some of these inspirational sayings committed to memory:

- *When the going gets tough, the tough get going.*
- *Quitters never win, and winners never quit.*
- *When life hands you a lemon, make lemonade.*

As much as we roll our eyes when we hear such sentiments, they wouldn't have reached the point of tiredness if they didn't contain nuggets of truth.

But the concept of grit requires us to move beyond aphorisms. It asks us to realistically confront the possibility of failure, which can weigh heavily upon our shoulders. We hold a range of negative potential outcomes in our hands, and there's no guarantee how things are going to turn out. I can attest to the fact that I've been there—and it's a scary place.

In those moments, the prospect of failure leaves us feeling vulnerable and perhaps even fearful. That's when grit forces us to admit that we're vulnerable to the world that lies beyond our control— and encourages us to take a step toward the unknown anyway. There's a wall ahead that needs to be climbed.

Of course, grit doesn't guarantee a happy ending. We might fall off that wall we're climbing and have to start again. We might stumble when taking a risk and pursuing a dream. We might fail in a business venture.

But as the legendary Hollywood figure Mary Pickford reportedly said, "This thing that we call 'failure' is not the falling down but the staying down."

It's the grit that enables us to get back on our feet—where we strive to stay for the long term.

I understand that the idea of faithfulness to our long-term goals can seem daunting. A New Year's resolution to lose weight is one thing, but it gets real when we're thinking about quitting a safe job and starting our own business.

I don't mean to say that our first implementation of the grit concept should prompt us to jump overboard in deep water and choppy waves—speaking metaphorically, of course. In the real world, that might equate to quitting a good job without coming up with a realistic plan for the next stage.

But I do want to suggest that we can start by working out our "grit muscle" in smaller, less- risky areas. We may decide to drive past the fast-food joint and buy healthy food at the grocery.

We may ask our children, spouse or friends what we can do to improve our relationships. We may choose to use the stairs rather than the elevator. To recharge our spiritual life, we may set the alarm clock for 20 minutes earlier every morning so we can spend some time with our Creator or write in a gratitude journal.

Even these kinds of everyday things take discipline. And as we do them, we'll be better equipped to employ grit when the stakes are higher. Eventually, we'll find that our "baby steps" have turned into impactful *strides* toward reaching our long- term goals.

'Getting on with it'

Naturally, we need to be honest and recognize that major successes normally don't happen overnight—although lightning can (and sometimes does) strike. Rather, we typically reach our goals in stages. It's grit that allows us to keep plugging away and achieve the incremental successes that eventually get us where we want to be.

Steven Pressfield published an insightful, often-quoted book titled *The War of Art*. He observed that something he labeled *Resistance* stands between the life we want to live and the life we actually live. How do we defeat this enemy? We get on with it.

"If you're feeling Resistance," he wrote, "the good news is, it means there's tremendous love there too. If you didn't love the project that is terrifying you, you wouldn't feel anything. The opposite of love isn't hate; it's indifference. The more Resistance you experience, the more important your unmanifested art/project/enterprise is to you—and the more gratification you will feel when you finally do it."

That kind of thinking—paired with grit—can help us move from contemplation to action. Let me ask you to stop and think about your own life. Where is your focus? What is it that you truly desire? What are you passionate about?

What we're striving for is the kind of extraordinary life that we all want, even though our ideas of the good life may be different. Some may crave globe-trotting excitement, others a quiet, contemplative life. Some may want to make a name for themselves in politics or business, while others find satisfaction in raising a family or serving the community.

However, if we're honest with ourselves, most of us probably would admit that there's a gap between where we are today and where we really want to be. And I'd like to suggest that one way to bridge the gap is to use the grit concept that we've been exploring throughout this chapter.

As you may suspect by now, I've been an avid golfer for a long time—more than 50 years,

in fact. And for a good number of those years, I've thought about the many parallels between the game of life and the game of golf.

Each of us have our own challenges, predicaments and problems—much like a typical round of golf. We try to avoid the hazards in golf—such as hitting the ball out of bounds, into the water or into the sand traps—just as in life we try to avoid pain, problems and all the other things we don't want to deal with.

But in order to realize our potential in the game of golf as well as in life, according to sports psychologist Bob Rotella, we need to cultivate the three Ds, the three Ps and the three Cs:

Desire, Determination, and Discipline
Persistence, Patience, and Practice
Confidence, Concentration, and Composure

I think those nine concepts can be summarized in one word—grit.

Bringing this first chapter to a close, I'd like to share a poem I learned as I went from door to door selling Bibles—and I still read it when I'm on the verge of quitting.

"Don't Quit"
by John Greenleaf Whittier

When things go wrong, as they sometimes will,
When the road you're trudging seems all uphill,
When the funds are low and the debts are high,
And you want to smile, but you have to sigh,
When care is pressing you down a bit,
Rest, if you must, but don't you quit.

Life is queer with its twists and turns,
As every one of us sometimes learns,

And many a failure turns about,
When he might have won had he stuck it out;
Don't give up though the pace seems slow—
You may succeed with another blow.

Often the goal is nearer than,
It seems to a faint and faltering man,
Often the struggler has given up,
When he might have captured the victor's cup,
And he learned too late when the night slipped down,
How close he was to the golden crown.

Success is failure turned inside out—
The silver tint of the clouds of doubt,
And you never can tell how close you are,
It may be near when it seems so far,
So stick to the fight when you're hardest hit—
It's when things seem worst that you must not quit.

CHAPTER TWO

GRATITUDE

"When you are grateful, fear disappears
and abundance appears."
—*Tony Robbins*

When was the last time you went outside to contemplate the night sky?

Sometimes I find myself peering up at the heavens, transfixed by the enormity of the universe. There's something about the sky that hits me right in the chest—*kerchunk*—and knocks the pride right out of me.

I exist on a little plot of land in North America, in the Northern Hemisphere of the Earth—the third rock from the sun, and the only planet in our solar system with oceans on its surface. We are alive because, providentially, the Earth's atmosphere is *precisely* that which is required for life. The world as we know it wouldn't exist if a vast array of elements hadn't been finely tuned to precise specifications. For example, our planet is the perfect distance from the sun. If we were any closer, we'd burn up. If we were a little farther away, we'd be frozen solid.

Scientists tell us that the odds of all the required specifications for life just happening to line up by chance are incomprehensibly small.

In the film "The Privileged Planet," researchers assert that the chances of life as we know it actually existing is "one one-thousandth of one one- trillionth." If we were missing only one element among the many, or if one element had been "tuned" in a slightly different way, the planet wouldn't be able to support life. *And we wouldn't even be here.* Gratitude is the appropriate response for what Guillermo Gonzalez and Jay W. Richards have called our "privileged planet."

Night or day, when I look up at the sky, I'm reminded how small I am. In my tiny corner of the universe, it can seem to me that my joys and problems are the only things in existence. But that couldn't be further from the truth.

No matter how much I try to wrap my head around the vastness of the universe, I simply can't do it. Astronomers say it would take 100,000 years for a traveler to cross our own Milky Way galaxy—and that's traveling at the speed of light, which covers 186,282 miles per second and nearly six trillion miles in a year. And those 100,000 years would get you across only one galaxy. How many galaxies are there? *Two trillion*, according to recent calculations. The scale of the universe is far beyond any human's ability to comprehend. It's something that strikes me with awe and keeps bringing me to my knees.

There are few things I love more than a clear night. I gaze at the sky and contemplate the constellations, planets and distant galaxies. The stars capture my imagination the most. I remember being in high school and visiting a planetarium for the first time—in a somewhat-altered state of mind.

That big ball came out of the floor and projected all the heavenly orbs onto the dome for us to observe. Wow—that was a mind-expanding experience. Later on in college, I took an astronomy course. I learned that even a little knowledge can immensely increase our appreciation for the cosmos.

Our eyes can take us only so far, just as our magnificent telescopes can't reveal the entire universe with clarity. Naturally, as technology advances and we push the frontiers of knowledge, we'll realize how little we know today. Astonishing things are beyond our current understanding, and as they're slowly revealed, we'll realize that there's yet more to be discovered.

And here I am, situated on planet Earth, overwhelmed by the vastness of creation—writing a book and trying to convey merely the tiniest fragment of the sense of awe, inspiration and gratitude that I feel.

Pointing a telescope toward the heavens and contemplating the universe can help us cultivate a greater awareness of the wonder of our existence. And that's a great way to start thinking about the focus of this chapter.

Looking inward

We also can point the telescope inward, so to speak, and take stock of how we live our lives in light of this important concept of gratitude. By the time you've finished reading this chapter, you'll understand how the steady cultivation of a sense of gratitude can transform the way we look at and experience the world.

Let's begin by recognizing that there are a lot of things we should be thankful for but never really take the time to appreciate. Sometimes those are the big things, like the universe that surrounds us. Other times, they can be the seemingly mundane things that aren't really mundane at all if we look at them in historical perspective.

For example, we expect the Wi-Fi to work and connect us to the world, the air conditioner to function when the temperature rises, and the family minivan to transport us where we're going without a mechanical breakdown. Although these technologies would have sounded miraculous not very many generations ago, today we complain mightily if any of them malfunction. But when they work properly day after day, we may never think to be grateful—we take them for granted.

Of course, the smartphones, computers and other gadgets of technological wizardry, as wonderful as they may be, aren't the first things we should be thankful for. We can—indeed, *we must*—develop a deeper sense of gratitude for the people who share our lives with us.

In that context, it's important for us as individuals to recognize that everything isn't about *me*. (I hadn't yet learned that lesson when I got ensnared in the "bowling alley adventure" I described in chapter one.) And a sense of gratitude will help us absorb the lesson that our friends, colleagues, family members and even casual acquaintances are on the same journey we're on— we're all trying to live our best lives.

One of the problems that has afflicted humankind since the beginning is that we tend to be selfish. It's as if we have blinders on and can't see the world from another's perspective. Even the ancient wisdom "Do to others as you would have them do to you" (Luke 6:31, NIV) often seems beyond our grasp.

The answer—and the challenge—is to scale the mountain, metaphorically speaking, and look down into the village, where we see others from a different vantage point. From this height, it's easier to be thankful for the value and the uniqueness of each individual. It's easier to be grateful for our human connections, our communities, our relationships. And it's easier for us to move beyond self-centeredness and ask, "What can I do to make that person's life better today?" When that happens, gratitude is channeled into positive action.

As we cultivate a greater sense of gratitude, let's take time to appreciate the people who live life alongside us.

Embracing gratitude

Through my reading, research and personal experiences, I've learned a great deal about how embracing gratitude can dramatically improve my life.

One helpful resource I encountered was a talk given on the TED-Ed platform by David Steindl-Rast, a monk and scholar.

In the talk, Steindl-Rast discusses something that he says we all have in common: the desire for happiness. It would be hard to argue with that idea, although we certainly define happiness in different ways. But how do we achieve happiness, and how does that state of mind relate to gratitude?

Many people mistakenly think that we become happy when we accumulate certain accomplishments or develop relationships with certain people or acquire certain possessions. (I hear that new sports car whispering in my ear right now.) Well, some of those things may be perfectly fine. But the point is that they don't yield lasting happiness.

Steindl-Rast reverses the whole equation. You might say that he turns the traditional "happiness formula" upside down. "It is not happiness that makes us grateful," he tells a group of attentive people in his TED-Ed audience. "It's gratefulness that makes us happy."

That's a revolutionary concept, isn't it? Well, actually—maybe it's not. You may recall that the Apostle Paul instructed the readers of one of his letters to give thanks "in all circumstances" (1 Thessalonians 5:18, NIV).

We view the world differently if we discipline ourselves to see our circumstances—whatever they may be—through the lens of gratitude.

The benefits of gratitude

It turns out that giving thanks is not just good theology. There's also emerging scientific evidence to support the claim that gratitude can in fact improve many aspects of our lives.

With the rise of positive psychology in recent decades, gratitude has become a powerful word and concept in the world of health—from the mental to the social to the physical realms. If you do a Google search for the word gratitude, you'll undoubtedly find a couple hundred million hits.

A recent article published by the Greater Good Science Center, associated with the University of California at Berkeley, started off with this report: "After 15 years of research, we know that gratitude is a key to psychological well-being. Gratitude can make people happier, improve their relationships, and potentially even counteract depression and suicidal thoughts."

What's more, the article pointed to evidence suggesting that the positive effects of gratitude also might carry over to one's physical health. "Gratitude...can be an incredibly powerful and invigorating experience," said Dr. Jeffrey Huffman, a researcher and professor at Harvard Medical School. "There is growing evidence that being grateful may not only bring good feelings. It could lead to better health."

For example, Dr. Huffman and a number of other researchers designed a study to investigate whether patients could more effectively recover from a heart attack if they cultivated a sense of gratitude. The study participants who were given "gratitude exercises" to do over a period of weeks fared much better than those who got the traditional treatment. The patients who wrote gratitude journals and letters, according to Dr. Huffman, "experienced much greater improvements in positive affect, anxiety, and depression." Subsequent research along those lines confirmed that gratitude among heart-attack patients was associated with "more positive feeling, healthier eating, and more physical activity, as well as less depression and anxiety."

Other studies have yielded similar results as the amount of research has multiplied on topics related to gratitude. In fact, there's an academic publication—titled *The Journal of Happiness Studies*—that frequently reports on the role of gratitude in human well-being.

In one study that the journal published, participants were given a six-week "gratitude intervention." They were assigned daily writing and reflection activities that focused their attention on the people, things, events and circumstances they were grateful for. At the end of the study, the researchers concluded that such a program could be an effective mechanism for improving an individual's sense of well-being. In addition, follow-up contact with the participants six months later suggested that the focus on gratitude could "promote a lasting appreciative perspective on life."

It will be interesting to see what future research brings to light about the positive effects of gratitude in our lives.

Putting gratitude into practice

But we don't need a heart attack, an academic study or a medical degree from Harvard to more effectively harness the power of gratitude for improved mental and physical health. We can do something as simple as write a letter of gratitude to a friend or loved one. Or we can start to keep a "gratitude journal." These are exercises—used in Dr. Huffman's research— that give us a good, practical way to develop a deeper sense of gratitude. Let's take a minute to drill down on the journals.

For about 10 years, a college professor near my home has been collaborating with her students on a gratitude journal that takes the form of a digital list that they maintain throughout the semester. At the beginning of each class session, Professor Deborah Miller Fox takes a moment for her students to share aloud a few things they're grateful for.

The English professor tells her students that this habit of regularly and publicly naming specific blessings helps them strike a mental posture that is essential for learning: humility. "Gratitude helps us to become teachable because it requires the humility of acknowledging another person's generosity in our lives," Professor Miller Fox explains.

Typically, she says, students start out being a little shy about participating, but after a few weeks of engagement, their enthusiasm invariably grows—particularly as the semester becomes more stressful. During the last two weeks of a recent semester, she reports, the students were so determined to see their gratitude list reach 1,000 blessings that they all made a pact to add multiple items to the list daily: "I'm grateful for the phone call from my mom last night." "I'm grateful for hot coffee this morning." "I'm grateful to Professor Jones for letting me make up the quiz I missed yesterday."

Many students end up feeling that the gratitude exercise was one of the most meaningful parts of the class. "We learn a great deal about each other from this list," says Professor Miller Fox, "and our time together is enriched by a practice that reminds us that even when we arrive to class thinking we have nothing to offer, there is always something for which to be thankful."

As that anecdote suggests, some people find it tremendously helpful to keep a daily journal about their gratitude. We don't have to write a dissertation—just a few words will do. And all we need is a notebook, a pen and the discipline to keep focusing on what we're thankful for. (If you prefer writing in pixels over writing with ink, you can use one of the many gratitude apps that have become available.)

If you really get into the journaling, you could dive in a little deeper. You could paint a picture for the cover, or you could create a gratitude scrapbook by cutting out photos from magazines or taking your own photos. You could start a blog to share with your friends and family. Or you could create a "jar of blessings" by writing what you're thankful for on scraps of paper and then depositing them in the jar every day.

Of course, if journaling isn't your style, you could verbalize what you're grateful for. Tell a friend or loved one, tell your small group, mention your gratitude to a colleague at work. You'll benefit—but your focus on gratitude could help change someone else's life as well.

The bottom line is that if we aren't writing down the things we're thankful for, we should make an effort to focus on them in another way—even if that involves just thinking about them while we take a walk, meditate or drive to the health club. We might even consider putting our socks under the bed when we turn in for the night. Then in the morning, we'll need to get down on our knees to retrieve them. In that humble position, we'll be reminded to breathe a prayer of gratitude for a new day.

Whatever the mechanisms you might choose for growing in gratitude, I hope your pursuit of a more-thankful life bleeds over into your daily activities. Volunteer at a school or non-profit. Devote some of your time to a cause other than yourself. Develop a new relationship that demands more of you than you're used to giving. The possibilities are limitless.

As you can see, cultivating a sense of gratitude doesn't require a lot of work, a stash of cash or a comprehensive plan. It just requires a new kind of focus.

An ever-present mindset

We're all human, and we all fall down on the job from time to time. It's not realistic to think that once we embrace gratitude, we'll never hit another pothole on the road of life. At least this is true in my case. To be honest, sometimes I'm not the best at being grateful.

When I'm having a stressful day or I get overwhelmed by circumstances, I may lose focus and drift away from the grateful, gracious and thoughtful mindset that I like to maintain. But I've tried to develop the ability to recognize in those moments that I'm nowhere close to being where I should be mentally and emotionally. That can help me get back on track more quickly.

So how do we react and return to a better headspace when we find ourselves veering off course? A strategy I typically use is to remember the Triangle Effect and how the power of three can get me back to where I need to be:

- *I stop.*
- *I take a deep breath.*
- *I contemplate three things I'm grateful for.*

Sometimes I think about my wife, children and grandchildren. Other times I think about the sun in the sky or my morning run. The beauty of this exercise is that it works every time. It jars me out of whatever negative mindset I've fallen into, and it prompts me to recalibrate my attitude.

Yes, it can be hard to make that transition in the moment when we're stressed out and dealing with a crisis at work or at home. Perhaps it's impossible to go take a walk in the park and contemplate life's blessings just when we need that kind of reflection the most.

But that's why it's important to live ever-present in a mindset of gratitude. If we daily pursue a life marked by appreciation, the stresses that we inevitably encounter won't have the power to knock us completely off course. We might get angry or frustrated, but we're less likely to sink into the quicksand of attitude meltdown and dysfunction.

Awareness, mindfulness, positive psychology—call it what you will, but the idea is to pay attention to (and of course be grateful for) what's truly important in life. I think a catchy, oft- quoted remark from Stephen Covey can be applied very effectively here: "The main thing is to keep the main thing the main thing."

A hard lesson

As I tried to suggest above, we're probably setting ourselves up for failure if we think a spirit of gratitude can inoculate us against life's turbulence. But even when we do fail, gratitude gives us a way to recover and carry on—we can learn from what we've done wrong.

Early in my career, I was excited to learn that the company I worked for was offering a fantastic sales incentive—a family vacation to Hawaii for insurance agents who achieved certain targets. Well, who wouldn't want to take a trip to Hawaii? I can say for sure that my wife did! So, brimming with energy and confidence at age 28, I figured I could hit those sales targets and score a trip to Aloha-land for my wife and me.

Denise and I shifted into serious planning mode as soon as the trip was announced. We actually had friends who lived in Hawaii, so we thought we'd extend the trip for another week and soak up every bit of sun and sand that we could. As the months went by, we got more and more excited about visiting the world-famous tropical paradise.

I really buckled down to make sure I was hitting the sales target, and I spent much of that year working six or seven days a week. I was on pace for the trip, a big bonus and a gold "honor ring" the company gave to its elite agents.

Everything was going great and according to plan—except for the fact that I did little but work for an entire year. And except for the fact that in November, a few of my clients canceled their life insurance policies. I scrambled to write more policies in a desperate attempt to stay on track for earning the trip, but a needed metric ratio was off.

Increasingly, it looked like my year-long labors would end up in exhaustion—and no trip to Hawaii. But I dutifully I set my alarm earlier, drank more coffee and kept my grinding goggles on.

By early December, I had managed to climb back to where I needed to be. I breathed a sigh of relief, but then, out of nowhere, I lost another policy. My manager told me that since it was a small juvenile policy that cost only $8 a month, I should sign the client's name on the reinstatement papers and pay for the policy myself. That way I could maintain the required ratio and preserve the trip to Hawaii.

I knew it was wrong. My conscience convicted me. But the pressure weighed heavily on my shoulders. How could I tell my wife that the trip was off and that she wouldn't be able to visit her best friend from high school? For that matter, how could I miss out on playing some of the most beautiful golf courses in the world with my best friend from college?

It was crunch time. Win or lose. All or nothing. I ignored my guilty feelings, signed the policyholder's name on the paperwork, sent in the payment and carried on with my work.

Later that month, I got a call from the home office. "The signatures don't match," the caller told me. I'll never forget what came next: I was about to be *terminated*. When the painful conversation ended, I felt almost suicidal for the first time in my life. "I hate myself," I thought.

I'd never felt more ashamed. In the following weeks, there were times I could barely breathe because of the tightness in my chest. I genuinely felt that I had signed away my life with the forged signature. I had lost everything—all for the shallow promise of a trip, a gaudy ring and a bonus check. Even as I relate this story, I can feel the stinging, burning sensation of my failure. No vacation was worth the mess I had created and the humiliation that followed.

I had to call my manager and explain what had happened. He went to bat for me by talking to higher-level managers, and he convinced them to let me keep my job. Talk about gratitude! I don't think I'd ever felt it more deeply.

Predictably, the stipulation was that I had to get the actual signature of the policyholder if I wanted to receive credit for the policy. Facing my shame head-on, I headed to the client's home in the middle of a snowstorm. She lived on the third floor of a rundown apartment complex. I knocked on the door.

The customer yelled, "Get out—I can't afford that policy!" I pleaded with her to let me in, and I told her my pathetic story. She was very gracious, and she signed the reinstatement form. Before I left, she looked at me and said, "Hey, send me a postcard from Hawaii."

And so, ultimately, Denise and I were able to take the trip we'd spent all year planning and anxiously awaiting. We had a lot of fun, at least on the surface. Underneath, though, I was still mired in shame as I contemplated a lesson I had learned the hard way.

A gratitude-first approach

The next year, I resolved to forget about the awards, the trips, the bonuses, the gold ring and the celebrations. It wasn't worth selling my soul to garner such rewards. Instead, I spent the year getting right with myself, right with my Creator and right with my relationship to work.

I felt tremendous gratitude to still have my job, and I made some life changes to make sure I could keep it. I made it a priority to have some quiet time, to keep a journal and to get in a good, long run before I started the workday. I even dusted off one of my old Bibles to read and study from cover to cover. (I actually followed a 52-week lesson plan that I had received as a gift during my college days as a Bible salesman.)

My new approach to work didn't have anything to do with time management, although I'm a big believer in that. Instead, it had everything to do with priorities. Mine were now set: body, mind and spirit. I had never before taken time for these priorities because I had always been rushing off to work.

But something amazing happened the next year. I fully expected that my productivity—sales and income—would drop because I was spending so much of my mornings exercising, getting my values and priorities in order, and getting my spiritual relationship with my Creator right. But the opposite happened. My productivity and income shot up. I was up nearly 30% over the prior year, in which I had worked 70 hours a week.

This was a paradigm shift for me—and one that I'm very glad to have experienced before I turned 30. The whole signature fiasco was a shock to my system, but it helped me get my priorities straight and feel true gratitude for the blessings of family and work that I've enjoyed ever since.

Gratitude in trying times

Gratitude is easy to come by when life is good: when your job is going well, when your kid gets a scholarship, when the doctor gives you a clean bill of health—and maybe especially when you just played a great round of golf.

But seriously, we all know that we can't camp up there on the mountaintop forever. I've made my living in the insurance business, so I'm well aware that disaster strikes. Accidents happen, homes burn down and people die unexpectedly. Some people end up isolated or abandoned and must walk alone. I think of people mired in abusive relationships, poverty, addiction, disease and hopelessness.

Does gratitude do us any good when it's hard to be grateful? When we're down in the valleys of life?

It's important to recognize that gratitude isn't a shield against the problems we confront. It isn't a mask that we put on to hide the pain and struggles that are taking place beneath the surface of our lives. It isn't a magic wand that makes our troubles go away.

Instead, it's a force that ushers us into a place of vulnerability and yet strength. It allows us to face difficult realities with an unexplainable courage. Perhaps most importantly, it gives us a sense of a broader, even eternal, perspective. It reminds us that our struggles, as real as they are to us, are subsumed by the grandeur of the universe and the love of our Creator. Gratitude opens our eyes to the reality that even in our smallness, we matter immensely, and nothing has the power to destroy us.

We've all been confronted by challenges, and many times they're truly daunting. But it's hard to imagine being worse off than a prisoner in a Nazi concentration camp during World War II.

That's where the Jewish psychiatrist Viktor Frankl found himself between 1942 and 1945. Naturally, the details of his imprisonment were horrific. He witnessed immense cruelty, he was tortured, and he never knew when he might instantly be put to death. His parents, his brother and his wife lost their lives in the camps.

But one day, alone and naked in a prison cell, he became aware that he had the ability to observe his life as if from another vantage point. He discovered that his identity and his power to choose how he responded to his circumstances were still intact. He decided that he wouldn't let his captors strip that power away from him. He used his mind and will to transform his existence into a source of strength. He even helped others find meaning in their suffering.

In a book he later wrote about his experience, Frankl looked back on his time in the concentration camp and identified sources of meaning that can be drawn upon when one starts to lose hope. And woven into his classic, oft-cited book was the idea that a sense of gratitude is essential to finding meaning even in the midst of great suffering.

A short summary like this can't really convey the depth of Frankl's insights in *Man's Search for Meaning*—one needs to read the entire work. But three quotations reveal the life-giving qualities that gratitude gave him even in the midst of the horror that he endured.

Wrote Frankl: "We who lived in concentration camps can remember the men who walked through the huts comforting others, giving away their last piece of bread. They may have been few in number, but they offer sufficient proof that everything can be taken from a man but one thing: the last of the human freedoms—to choose one's attitude in any given set of circumstances, to choose one's own way."

And in another memorable passage, he wrote: "We were grateful for the smallest of mercies. We were glad when there was time to delouse before going to bed, although in itself this was no pleasure, as it meant standing naked in an unheated hut where icicles hung from the ceiling. But we were thankful if there was no air raid alarm during this operation and the lights were not switched off. If we could not do the job properly, we were kept awake half the night."

A third and final quotation from the book has been in my collection since the beginning. It points to how gratitude motivates the best in us: "The more one forgets himself—by giving himself to a cause to serve or another person to love— the more human he is and the more he actualizes himself."

Gratitude and grace

Even in the worst circumstances we can imagine, gratitude provides a ray of hope and illuminates the path forward. It's possible to sustain deep gratitude for life's gifts even amidst the horror and cruelty of a concentration camp.

To be sure, gratitude can't solve every problem. Some issues require more than a grateful heart. But in every situation, gratitude serves as an important foundation.

Using the Triangle Effect, we can see that gratitude has beneficial, spiritual and transcendent qualities. It illuminates how our Creator is the ultimate giver, and the only response to these gifts is humility, wonder and a deep desire to give thanks. The more I acknowledge this undeserved kindness—or grace— the more it abounds. I'm astonished to continually see how gratitude brings more and more grace into my life.

Gratitude is a powerful concept and a worthwhile practice for all of us.

CHAPTER THREE

GOALS

"Goals are just dreams with deadlines."
—*Napoleon Hill*

If we managed our lives wisely, we'd invest more time in thinking about the kind of future we want to build. We wouldn't neglect the important task of visualizing what we want our lives to be like 10, 20 or even (if you're young enough) 50 years down the road.

The problem is that we often become so entrenched in the here and now that we fail to board an imaginary flight and look at our lives from that 30,000-foot cruising altitude. Instead—to switch analogies in mid-flight—the concerns of our day-to-day lives attach themselves to us like barnacles on a ship's hull. They're under the water line, so to speak, and we may not be conscious of their effects—but they surely will interfere with our ability to reach the destinations that we ought to be sailing to. Further, some of us are dragging along "anchors" that are making our voyages that much more difficult. Wouldn't it be great to clean off the barnacles and cut loose the anchors? This chapter moves us squarely in that direction.

It's easy to fall into the trap of short-sighted living. We can get so immersed in the worries, concerns and priorities of the day that we neglect the long-term things that are more important— such as growing as a person and shaping the kind of future that we'd like to live in. We get so laser-focused on what's demanding our attention right now that we literally forget about our hopes, dreams and goals. And it happens so quickly.

Maybe we've been in a super busy season at work. We have to put in some overtime, pick up the slack for a sick colleague or burn the midnight oil on a project that the boss needed yesterday. Well, we all want to be good employees, so chances are that we stay on the hamster wheel and do what needs to be done. The demands of the day take priority.

What happens to our life goals then—if indeed we ever found time to set them? We tell ourselves we don't have time to work on them right now, but we'll get to them eventually. And it becomes easier and easier, as the days and years go by, to put personal, big-picture goals on the back burner...and forget all about them.

We end up neglecting the things that are essential to growth— such as practicing awareness, articulating our goals and commitments, and developing strategies for where we want to be. Next thing you know, we're buried in an avalanche of daily demands. We get stuck going through the motions. Our lives in this state begin to feel normal, familiar and comfortable, so we're not motivated to change. We fail to grow. We start to become a lesser version of our authentic self. It's natural that our brain doesn't like uncertainty. We prefer what's familiar because certainty initiates a reward response, whereas uncertainty initiates a flight or fight response.

When we focus on something unfamiliar, our sympathetic nervous system prepares our mind and body to deal with the potential threat.

I've been there—and I can feel the anxiety building within me just *thinking* about this downward spiral.

The role of reflection

This takes us to some very important questions. How do we step out of this limiting, self- defeating mindset and step into our true calling? How do we find the time to pursue our higher aspirations? How do we grow, reach for our goals and follow our dreams when there's so much noise in our head—and a work project to complete, children to care for, a lawn to mow, bills to pay, a car to repair?

This is the time to hit the pause button and call a time-out. Close your eyes. Breathe deeply. Let go of the tension. Visualize three blessings in your life and hold them close for a moment. And reflect on the fact that it's possible to take control of your story.

That kind of reflection enables us to see things more clearly. It's kind of like the process that takes place when we have to start up the car and it has a frosted-over windshield. We can't just take off driving—we won't be able to see the road. We need to let the defroster do its work. In the same way, taking time out for reflection cleans off the windshield of our perspective.

If our subconscious mind can be programmed, it also can be reprogrammed. This is a very important concept to grasp, and we'll examine it in detail in later chapters. But when we change our story, we change our life. We can add plot twists to the narrative we've been living. Maybe we can't change the *beginning* of the story, but we can write the current chapter and the ending to reflect the outcome we want.

But really—how do we make plans and stick with them? How can we get the urgent stuff done while reaching for the stars? How can we become powerful through our ability to remain focused and goal-oriented?

If we don't get a handle on those kinds of questions, it's going to be difficult to achieve a balanced and extraordinary life. But every single person is capable of living a *today life* while reaching for a *tomorrow dream.* Yes, it's possible to live fully today while also reaching for our ideal tomorrow.

The snooze-button decision

The transformation begins with every principle outlined in *The Triangle Effect.* Each chapter holds a key to making us more powerful—in all the right ways. When we take steps each day to improve ourselves in the here and now, we're investing in a brighter, healthier, more-powerful future. What I invest in myself today will multiply tomorrow.

If we're investing in the snooze button, then guess what? We won't make much progress toward our higher priorities. If we're investing in griping about our morning commute or the bad drivers we encounter, we're actually investing in a lousy attitude, an angry spirit and a low-power life.

We won't accomplish anything if we're investing in negative thoughts, negative behaviors and negative judgments. Instead, we'll be sliding backward. It sometimes can be tempting to feel like a victim, but complaining about life circumstances is a strategy that never works. It takes courage and discipline, but we have the ability to change our story, change our choices and change our habits—which will then change our life.

The process of change can begin tomorrow morning when the alarm clock rouses us from our slumber. We can resist the temptation to hit that snooze button and catch a little more shut- eye. Instead of sleeping in, we can resolve to stand up and begin the day within five seconds of the time the alarm sounds.

This five-second idea comes from life coach and motivational speaker Mel Robbins, who authored a book about this concept—called *The 5 Second Rule.*

Essentially, Robbins contends that when there's something we know we need to do, we have five seconds to act before our brain pulls the emergency brake and shuts the process down. If we don't act immediately, the chances are that we won't act at all.

"Hesitation is the kiss of death," Robbins says. "You might hesitate for just a nanosecond, but that's all it takes. That one small hesitation triggers a mental system that's designed to stop you. And it happens in less than—you guessed it—five seconds."

In reality—for me, at least—it takes only three seconds to capture a thought and determine if I should move ahead with some kind of action. Of course, that fits with my theme of "the power of three." Granted, I probably can't persuade Robbins to change the title of her bestselling book to *The 3 Second Rule*, but you get the point.

We may not want to roll out of bed right away. We may not want to tackle a tricky home-maintenance project. We may not want to get our affairs in order for our family because we don't like talking about possible sickness or death.

But there's some good news. If we can act quickly—using that advice from Mel Robbins—we can begin to make those course changes that get us past what's easy in this moment and move toward the goals that will pay off tomorrow and in all the tomorrows to come.

Our thoughts, state of mind and angle of perception must change. The barnacles need to be scraped off. So, let's get moving.

Goals must take physical form

In the remainder of this chapter, we'll work on setting goals that are achievable. But underlying all of these techniques is the idea that our goals have to take written form.

Now, you'll notice that I used the word "setting" in that previous paragraph. I did that intentionally to evoke the image of setting type.

Young people may not have any idea what typesetting means. But many guys my age who took shop class in high school learned the old-fashioned art and technique of printing—pretty much the way Gutenberg did it back around 1450. The idea was to take characters made of metal, arrange them in words and sentences in a "job case," apply ink, and run sheets of paper through the printing press.

But there was nothing tentative about a block of set type. It was heavy. It formed a solid matrix. And it made an impression—literally—when it was pressed to paper.

That's what our goals should be like. Yes, our goals will change as we reach new insights and life stages—the goals you set when you're 25 wouldn't be the same ones you set when you're 45 or 65. But my point is that they need to be written down in order to be actionable.

It doesn't really matter if we write our goals in a notebook, scratch them out on the back of a napkin, use the pixels in a smartphone app or even use old-fashioned printing methods— which is unlikely, although you perhaps could find the antique equipment on eBay.

But our goals must be written down in one way or another. If they take up residence only in our brain cells, it won't be long before they move out. *Written goals are power.*

The "Yale study of goals" refers to a now-legendary story about the importance of creating detailed plans to guide our futures. Here's how Fast Company described it:

"In 1953, researchers surveyed Yale's graduating seniors to determine how many of them had specific, written goals for their future. The answer: 3%. Twenty years later, researchers polled the surviving members of the Class of 1953—and found that the 3% with goals had accumulated more personal financial wealth than the other 97% of the class combined!"

Fast Company tried to trace the lineage of the story, which has been told for years by motivational and productivity figures such as Tony Robbins, Brian Tracy and Zig Ziglar. Fast Company asked Robbins about the study, and his office referred them to Tracy. Tracy referred them to Ziglar, who in turn sent them back to Robbins. It turned out to be a kind of Triangle Effect loop.

Although Fast Company couldn't confirm that the Yale study ever took place, it's an interesting tale to contemplate—and even if it's apocryphal, it helps us focus on the importance of having thoughtful, written goals.

Consider the purpose

We'll get to writing our goals before long. But first, we need to do some very important spadework. We need to ask the question, To what end? What is the ultimate purpose of our goal setting?

We can have a comprehensive list of forward-thinking, carefully written goals—but first we need be clear about the destination we want to reach. To use a travel analogy, if we want to take a vacation in Switzerland, we don't want to set goals that have us landing at the airport in Jamaica. 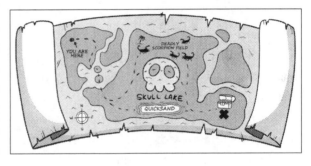 We can have a perfectly good vacation in Jamaica—but if our intention is to rent a chalet and do some skiing, we better have goals that will get us to the Swiss Alps instead.

I like to think of this process in terms of a pirate's treasure map. To find the buried chest of gold, we need to know three things: the starting point ("you are here"), the path and hazards along the way, and finally the location of the treasure ("x marks the spot").

To follow through with that analogy, here are the three questions we need to answer:

- *Do we really know who we are and where we are on the map of life?*

- *Do we have a roadmap or a plan?*
- *Are we clear on what our treasure/vision really is? Making goals quantifiable*

Goal setting can be simple enough when we're talking about achievements that are easily observable and measurable. For example, I've spent my career in the world of business, finance and sales, so I'm comfortable with setting goals that focus on things like expanding the customer base, increasing sales and boosting profit margins. I'm very grateful I learned these skills early in life.

In the insurance business, my company used to require us to periodically submit a written sales goal to the manager. To keep us on track, some of us then would make a fake sales commission check—we'd never try to cash it, of course!—in the ambitious amount that we hoped it would be. That would give us a goal to keep us motivated. We'd put the "check" on the car's dashboard, on the bathroom mirror, on the refrigerator and in other places where we could see it all the time. The motto was, "If you can see it, you can achieve it."

Naturally, the kinds of goals that we can formulate are limited only by our imaginations. A young couple might aim to save enough money for the down payment on a house. A college student might aspire to bump up the GPA from 3.2 to 3.5 next semester. Someone who wants to get in better shape might resolve to lose a certain amount of weight. A too-busy parent might make a promise to spend more time with the children each week.

One thing you'll notice about these goals is that they're all quantifiable. We can set and measure them. We can look at the numbers in a savings account or on a weight scale in the gym to determine whether we're making progress toward attaining those goals.

Now, some of the goals we come up with might not be quite so quantifiable. For example, we might start the new year with a resolution to be happier, to be kinder, to have a more positive attitude or to be more spiritually connected. Those are all desirable goals, but if we don't attach some markers or numbers to them, we might find it difficult to stay on track and know if we're making progress.

The idea is to be able to judge by an objective standard whether we're achieving the kind of results we want to see. Remember, abstract and subjective goals can be elusive. We want to formulate our goals in terms that can be observed and measured.

Use the reticular activating system

My experience has taught me a very interesting thing that pertains to our ability to set and reach goals. It involves the human brain's "reticular activating system" (RAS). This is a bundle of nerves located in the brainstem, and in layman's terms, it's kind of like "air traffic control" for most of the information that enters our brains.

Consider the vast amount of information that can enter our minds at any given moment. In this stimulus-rich world, our five senses can take in millions of bits of data per second. But let's say you're a spectator at a Little League baseball game. What are you paying attention to? Your child or grandchild, of course. Are you hearing the chirping of birds, the rustling of leaves or the sound of traffic on a nearby highway? Probably not.

It's the reticular activating system that filters out the extraneous stuff that doesn't pertain to our priorities at any given moment. Without this system, we'd be overwhelmed by all the stimuli that our senses could perceive.

An article on Beliefnet entitled "Train Your Brain to Manifest For You" put it this way:

"The reticular activating system acts like a gatekeeper or a bouncer at a loud, crowded bar. It decides what information gets into your brain and subconscious and what information, events and experiences are kept out. Your RAS looks for situations that will validate and prove your beliefs. It filters out things that don't fit within your spectrum of beliefs."

Awareness of the reticular activating system is the key to controlling the ideas that take precedence in our minds. Do we want to have a self-defeating attitude or a mindset that envisions positive possibilities? If the latter, we need to make the RAS work for us.

When we commit to a goal or plan, we create a mental picture of it. In a manner of speaking, we live the event before it happens. As we focus on this picture as being achievable, our RAS can seek out positive, empowering information and feed that into our mind. The process makes it much more likely that we can achieve our goals.

By the same token, a negative focus can take us down the opposite path. If we're constantly telling ourselves that we're not good at math or public speaking or relationships, we're setting ourselves up for failure. I think there's a lot of truth in the idea that, as the Beliefnet article expressed it, "Self-talk leads to belief which programs the RAS to deliver proof of your beliefs."

How can we make the reticular activating system contribute to our ability to reach our goals? We can constantly envision the things we want to achieve—and act *as if* they're coming to pass. Hang a poster on the office wall. Put a sticky note on the dashboard and computer screen. Use a phone app to send ourselves daily reminders that we'll get to the place we want to be.

My personal choice has been to write my goals (as well as some affirmation statements to keep me motivated) on 3x5 cards so I can carry them with me wherever I go. But whatever the techniques we use, we need to envision positive outcomes and live as though reaching our goals is a done deal.

To be the very best version of ourselves, we need a detailed plan or set of instructions to guide us in getting from where we are to where we want to be. This detailed plan is our treasure map, which allows us to organize our thinking so we can do what's necessary to reach our goals.

Step one: Self-awareness and discovery

I've been a goal-setter for decades, and for me the whole point has been to find the power I need to live the kind of life I desire. I'd like to share a three-point goal-setting system that has worked for me. I'm confident it'll work for you, too. The first step involves a process of self- awareness and discovery.

As we approach the goal-setting runway, it's important to take some time to engage in a period of reflection that will yield smarter, wiser goals. This topic will come up again, but I recommend that we begin with a personal "mission statement" for life. Naturally, such a statement should bring into sharp relief our convictions about what we're on the planet to achieve. The key question is, *What is the main purpose of my life?* Understanding our overarching purpose is central to the goal-setting task at hand.

Once we've crafted our mission statement, we can drill down to the next level and identify the kinds of things that are important to us and that feed into our goal-setting.

We've all heard the phrase "Know thyself," which Socrates supposedly delivered to his followers. The ancient philosopher clearly wasn't thinking in terms of modern goal-setting theory when he uttered those words, but the directive makes a lot of sense in the context that we're presently working in. After all, wouldn't it be a major waste of time and effort to write life goals without understanding our values, aptitudes, strengths and weaknesses?

Although we undoubtedly have an innate sense of what our values are, I think it can be helpful to put them in writing. This brings them to the forefront of our mind as we work on setting our goals.

Writing down goals is not a new concept. Back in the 1700s when he was just 21 years old, Benjamin Franklin developed a step-by-step system to help him achieve the things he wanted to achieve in life. In his autobiography, he listed 13 virtues that he intended to cultivate. He then developed a virtue-tracking journal so he could practice those virtues daily. I've used a version of this system over the years and have found it to be a great way to maintain a strong moral compass in my own life.

Another simple but worthwhile exercise is to find already existing lists of values. Such lists can help us identify the values that matter most to us.

Let's take a list from *Psychology Today* as an example (see Appendix A). Among the 39 values listed there are some that I tend to gravitate toward—learning, growth and spirituality. I'd be surprised if any two readers of this book came up with exactly the same list, but what matters is that we're being reflective about our life's highest values so that our goals can reflect them.

Here's an action step that you can take right now. Think about some of your personal values.

If you need some ideas, go to Appendix A. Record your top three values here:

1)
2)
3)

Next, transfer those values and what they mean to you to a 3x5 card and carry them with you for three days—reading and contemplating them three times a day. You'll be amazed at the results. Continue this for three weeks, and you'll be changed. Continue for three months, and you'll be transformed. This kind of exercise helps us build awareness of how our lives move in harmony with our values—and sometimes, perhaps, how they don't. It's a simple exercise, but it's one that can be valuable in identifying and cultivating the values that we want to live by.

That's just one method for getting a better grasp on our core values. But the values- identification process is critically important because we can't effectively set goals without knowing what drives our behaviors and attitudes.

Identifying our character strengths

Someone who really wants to take a deep dive into the power of values should consider visiting the website of the VIA Institute on Character—easily found online. The organization offers a free survey tool that's based on "a common language of 24 character strengths." People who take the survey are able to determine their individual "character-strengths profile."

These VIA strengths include values that are cited often within *The Triangle Effect*. Since these character strengths are the basic elements of our identity, we need to spend time understanding which ones are most reflected in our individual lives. It's important for us to identify our top three as well as our bottom three.

The book *The Power of Character Strengths*, which builds on the VIA values, notes that your personal mix of character strengths is almost certainly unique to you. Why? Because when you do the math, you'll see that the 24 items in the test yield "over 600 sextillion possible combinations." Taking time to understand our unique character strengths can help us write more realistic and relevant goals.

Another notable insight of the book pertains to character strengths and "the three Es." Our top-three character strengths will become *essential* to our identities. It will feel *effortless* for us to employ or enact these strengths. And when we use these strengths, they will *energize* us.

Wouldn't you agree that it's important to know what our unique character strengths are before we start setting life goals?

For extra credit, power and awareness, try giving family members and friends a list of the 24 character strengths—and let them tell you which ones they think are your top three.

Why we work

Since working is a big part of most people's lives, I always ask the question, *Why do we work?* If you take a look at Appendix B, you'll find a list of 17 possible reasons that people work. Once you've reflected on the matter, list the top three reasons that you, personally, punch the clock or earn a salary:

1)
2)
3)

Many people don't really understand why they work—or at least they don't make a conscious connection between how they earn a living and the values that are important to them. Sometimes there can be a pretty big disconnect between these areas, but it's critically important for them to be in congruence. If they're not, our work isn't likely to be fulfilling. It's a good idea for us to think seriously about our values and how we live our lives—and even to revisit those issues from time to time as the years go by.

As we'll see in the Balance chapters, there are healthy as well as unhealthy ways to engage in our work. But eventually we'll clock out—or perhaps our life circumstances don't have us working at all. When this is the case, we still want to live in a way that's congruent with our values. Again, it's a good idea to identify the values that we want to incorporate into the goals that pertain to our personal time, family relationships, travel, hobbies, community activities, volunteer work and so on.

Avoiding regrets

In 2009, an Australian caregiver by the name of Bronnie Ware wrote a blog post about her experiences with hospice patients. As they approached life's end, these dying individuals told Ware what they wished they had done differently in their lives. The authentic, honest conversations that resulted became the basis for Ware's article "Regrets of the Dying," which took the world by storm and gave her an international platform for writing books and sharing how people could live, as she puts it, "a regret-free life that not only honors your heart's calling, but has the potential to impact the lives of those near and far."

And what were the top five regrets of the dying?

- *I wish I'd had the courage to live a life true to myself, not the life others expected of me.*
- *I wish I hadn't worked so hard.*
- *I wish I'd had the courage to express my feelings.*
- *I wish I had stayed in touch with my friends.*
- *I wish that I had let myself be happier.*

By drawing on that list—or by coming up with your own ideas—name the three regrets that you want to avoid having later in life:

1)
2)
3)

We need to remember that one or more of those regrets might eventually become reality for us if we don't make conscious choices—work-related and otherwise—at this stage of our lives.

This awareness and self-discovery step can be a very "get real" and sobering event for your life. Also, it can have a tremendous effect on your life now and in the future—as well as on the people around you.

Rick Warren said in his famous book, *The Purpose Driven Life*: "The fear of what we might discover if we honestly faced our character defects keeps us living in the prison of denial."

To become the best humans we can become, we must be truly honest with ourselves. In the process, we need to be mindful of how bad decisions could lead to future regrets. There is power in understanding possible regrets, and looking backwards can actually move us forward in a more powerful way. Let me give you an example that has been circulated widely, even though some of the story's veracity may be in dispute.

One morning in 1888, when Swedish chemist and inventor Alfred Nobel was reading the morning newspaper, he was surprised to encounter his own obituary. The headline read "The merchant of death is dead," and the article noted that Nobel had become fabulously wealthy by inventing dynamite and selling weapons of war.

However, the newspaper had mistakenly identified Alfred as the deceased. In actuality, his brother Ludwig was the one who had died. But when Alfred saw how the article described what his legacy was shaping up to be, he resolved to make some changes. He decided that he wanted to be remembered not as a warmonger but as a humanitarian.

When he died eight years later, Alfred Nobel left his entire estate not to his family but to a fund that would honor the people who would make the greatest contributions to mankind in any given year. Ever since, Nobel Prizes have been awarded annually to noteworthy people who have made important contributions in areas such as peace, physics, chemistry and medicine.

We may not have the experience of reading our own obituary and then reorienting our lives.

However, intentional discovery of our personal character flaws could have a major impact on us as well as the people around us and the universe we find ourselves in. Taking this kind of self- inventory with a close friend, a professional or a small group could switch on our brains to more power, balance and energy.

Now, it's not realistic to think that we can cross the finish line with absolutely no regrets. If you and I were to meet for a cup of coffee, we'd undoubtedly have many regrets to share with each other. But being reflective and setting goals for the future can set us up to live the kind of life that this entire book points to—one that is thoughtful, filled with joy and motivated by purpose.

Step two: Brainstorming

Once the discovery journey has given us the kind of self- awareness we need about our values and ultimate purpose, the next step in the process is brainstorming.

Take out a notebook or open an app on your favorite electronic device. Start writing down goals that you might want to consider. Anything is possible at this point—don't place artificial limits on yourself, and don't reject a possible goal just because you might think it's not realistic financially or otherwise.

Ask yourself questions like these:

- What would you like to see happen in your life?
- What would you like to accomplish?
- What are the top 10 things on your bucket list?
- What's important to you in every area of your life—professionally, personally, spiritually?
- What type of person do you want to be?
- What character traits would you like to have?
- What character traits would you *not* like to have?
- What do you want your family life to be like?
- Where do you want to be in 10 or 20 years?
- What does your "retirement" look like?
- What's the plan for your end-of-life stage?
- What would you like people to say about you at your funeral?

We shouldn't attempt to write even a rough draft of our life goals in the time it takes to do a morning run or even binge- watch all the episodes of a favorite streaming show. The process requires time. Actually, we might need a few weeks—or even months—to do this right because the brainstorming needs to be based on some serious reflection.

When I've worked through this process, I've often tried to promote clear thinking by taking long walks or sitting in a comfortable chair in a quiet spot. I equip myself with some 3x5 cards and a pen. I never want to let a great idea slip away, so I write it down. Brainstorming can be compared to the process of creating art—we let it flow naturally without rushing. Some say this is where the everyday meets the divine.

A good example of a brainstorming goal-setter is Lou Holtz. When he was 28, he had just gotten fired from an assistant coaching job and was sitting at the kitchen table with his wife, who was pregnant with their third child. His wife gave him a book to help him out of the low-power state he was in.

The book was titled *The Magic of Thinking Big*, and Holtz took the goal-setting chapter very seriously. He went on to write out 107 things he wanted to accomplish in his life. They included meeting the pope, winning a national championship, coaching Notre Dame football, being a guest on "The Tonight Show" and having dinner at the White House. At last count he had reached 102 of his original 107 goals.

It would be perfectly sensible to discuss goal-setting with family members and perhaps even close friends. They might be able to impart some wisdom that we'd otherwise miss.

Perhaps we can achieve some additional insight by going through the family archives and photo albums and remembering our roots. Think about the milestones along your journey thus far. Look ahead and review your retirement plan. If one of your long-term goals is to do some serious boating, get some brochures showing the kind of watercraft you might want to buy. If you want to do a lot of overseas traveling and take some mission trips, collect some very specific information. Remember, your reticular activating system can be harnessed in this effort.

If we were to embark on a risky new business venture, logic would say that we should very carefully think through the risks and rewards. Many successful companies do just that using what's called a "SWOT analysis." They brainstorm *strengths, weaknesses, opportunities* and *threats*.

I recommend that goal-oriented people do essentially the same thing by conducting a "personal SWOT analysis." Go ahead and name, in each of the sections below, your top three personal:

Strengths

1)
2)
3)

Weaknesses

1)
2)
3)

Opportunities

1)
2)
3)

Threats

1)
2)
3)

Refer to these insights as you brainstorm your goals. Just remember that this kind of brainstorming isn't a once-and-done process. My practice is to do this annually. I normally use the time between Thanksgiving and Christmas to take stock of where I am and formulate goals for the next year—and modify my longer-term goals as necessary. This ritual helps me start each January with a clear sense of vision.

Step three: Finalize your goals—and commit to them

If we follow the plan I've provided in the first and second stages of the goal-setting process, we'll now have a comprehensive list of ideas to work with as we formalize and finalize our goals in this third stage.

There are many techniques for setting and tracking our goals—perhaps even hundreds of them. You'll find workbooks, planners, smartphone apps and just about any other kind of goal- setting aid you can imagine. You don't have to choose a resource that's technologically sophisticated or has a "name brand" attached to it, although some of the packages are well designed and highly attractive.

The important thing is to engage in the process of thinking deeply, articulating our goals and tracking our progress. What specific tool we end up using is a matter of personal preference. If we're thoughtful and diligent in our goal-setting, we could get the job done with a small deck of 3x5 cards.

But I want to equip you with a specific toolkit, so I'll choose what's known as the SMART system. The acronym stands for:

- *Specific*
- *Measurable*
- *Achievable*
- *Relevant*
- *Time-based*

Actually, some authors will change the words a little bit to reflect their own emphases. For example, someone might use *affordable* instead of *achievable*. But the overall system provides a useful framework, even if there's a little variation from model to model.

Let me give you a brief overview of this system. The first letter in SMART stands for *specific*. It's important for our goals to have this characteristic so our minds can formulate a precise picture of what we're aiming for. Cloudy conceptualization leads to a cloudy future. We, in contrast, are after clarity and specificity. Do we want to "save enough money so I can retire early"—or do we want to "accumulate $1.5 million in a well- balanced retirement portfolio so I can move on to the next stage in my life on the day I turn 60"?

We all have many different hats that we wear in our journeys, so when we're writing goals, we need to be specific about the things we want to accomplish as a husband, wife, parent, grandparent, student, professional, volunteer, business owner, community member—whatever role we play. There's a place in this framework for goals like writing a book, earning an advanced degree or running a marathon.

Next, goals must be *measurable*, or else we won't know if we're actually making progress.

Making a goal measurable requires another M—*metrics*. What are the metrics we'll use to determine if we're on track—annual income, net worth, pounds, muscle mass, time units? Whenever possible, we want to attach measurable objectives to our goals.

Here's a very simple example. Let's say a life-insurance sales agent wants to earn $100,000 next year. The income goal for each month of the year would be $8,333. Now the agent has something both specific and measurable to guide her work. If she finds herself at the end of April, the fourth month, having earned only $25,000, she can tell that she's a month behind. By the same token, if she has accumulated sales commissions of $42,000 by then, she'll see that she's on the path to success.

Another important element of the SMART approach is that the plan should be *achievable*.

An unrealistic goal will promote discouragement, not inspire motivation. It follows that if we set a goal too low, we may not be challenged to fulfill our true potential.

We need to look at our goals with clear-eyed realism. It's good to have "stretch goals," but we need to make sure that we aren't thinking and dreaming unrealistically. For example, an NFL lineman who weighs 300 pounds probably shouldn't be contemplating a second career as a horse-racing jockey. Neither should the jockey think about trying to make a living as a middle linebacker in a professional football stadium!

Continuing with the model, goals also should be *relevant* to the purpose of our life. Here we again encounter the mission statement that we discussed earlier. Do the goals that we're writing align with the purposes that we feel we're on the planet to achieve? We need to think expansively here. Remember that our purposes are far greater than just personal fulfillment and happiness. I believe we all want to make our world a better place, so our goals should reflect that kind of relevance.

Now let's come back around to the quotation we began the chapter with: "Goals are just dreams with deadlines." This oft- cited adage drives home the importance of attaching a specific time frame to our goals. This is of course the last letter and the *time-based* element of the SMART model.

Our insurance agent from a few paragraphs ago didn't neglect the time dimension. She had a goal for every month, and those goals fed into a goal for an entire year. Even if we don't set a specific day-and-date deadline and instead prefer to work with a more general time frame (such as "retirement years"), we still need to feel a sense of urgency about getting things done on a specific timetable. Otherwise, our goals are likely to fade away and be forgotten.

For that reason, I encourage people to make deadlines or time frames an important part of the goals they write. What's the target date for saving up that 20% for the down payment on the house? What do we want to have our weight down to three months from now? This is another reason to put our goals in writing. That enables us to refer to them often and stay on track.

The traditional 3x5 cards always have worked well for me because I can put the goal on one side of the card then list all the reasons why reaching that goal is important on the back. I have an old cassette tape recording in which Jim Rohn, a motivational speaker and writer, said, "You can get yourself to do about anything you want if you give yourself enough reasons to do so."

Before we leave the time-based element, we should make a mental note that it can be helpful to think in terms of a goal- making trinity, so to speak. We want to have some short-range goals to hold ourselves accountable in the here and now— which I define as the year ahead. We need some mid-range goals for more than one year but less than five years out. And we need some long-range goals to keep us on track for five years or more—or even over the span of an entire lifetime.

Once again, it's not the *system* we use that matters. There's nothing magical about the SMART model or any of the others. What's important is the fact that we're contemplating what we want out of life and are planning the necessary strategy and steps to get there.

When we get off track

Once we have a set of life goals, we need to keep them close at hand. I like the idea of placing them on the refrigerator or in a prominent location in a workspace. At a minimum, we should set a calendar reminder to review our goals at specified time intervals.

But life circumstances change, and sometimes they change dramatically, so the plan we devise today might have to be revisited down the road. And even if our life remains pretty consistent for a long period of time, we'll no doubt have new visions and dreams that we want to incorporate into new or revised goals—so we never want to write our goals in indelible ink.

As I reflect on my own life, I become aware that I can sometimes get off track in terms of meeting my goals. Actually, I've been so far off so many times that I can't even begin to count them.

This is why I find it valuable to occasionally have a "get real with myself" talk. I take out a notebook and pen, and I revisit my goals. For me, this might be prompted by a life milestone or by ending a quarter during which I didn't meet my sales goals or some personal goal. What's essential is staying engaged in serious thought about our goals and ultimately our life's purpose.

It occurs to me that our ongoing goal-setting process is a lot like what happens in the navigation of a jet plane. At the beginning of a flight, all the appropriate data is entered into the system so the pilot can get the aircraft where it needs to go. But then during the flight, any number of factors—jet streams, for example, or the need to circumvent a big storm—have the potential to take the flight off course. The GPS system helps the pilot make incremental corrections along the way until the destination is reached.

We can think of our life journey in much the same way. We need to have a clear destination in mind, and then we may need to make adjustments as our life circumstances and our goals change. Just remember that the goal-setting process can help us think "big picture" with respect to our destination coordinates, and our God-given GPS system—our conscience, our thoughtfulness, our desire to do the right thing—helps us make necessary adjustments along the way.

I hope my three-point system for goal-setting will equip readers with some of the tools, keys and solution strategies needed to navigate life. After all, life has a way of moving through different seasons, and we can't stop our world from sometimes feeling out of control, confusing and crazy. We'll tackle this issue head-on in the book's next major section, Balance.

PART II

BALANCE

As you know by now, *The Triangle Effect* has three principal themes: Power, Balance and Energy. Now we move into that second section about balance.

If you think back to your childhood, you'll realize that you didn't have to stray very far from your baby crib to start getting a sense of how balance works. Every child knows the tale of "Goldilocks and the three bears."

In the classic narrative, the young, cottage-invading Goldilocks had a hard time finding food and furnishings to her liking. The porridge she wanted to eat was too hot or too cold, and the beds she wanted to nap in were too hard or too soft. But eventually, of course, Goldilocks found that the baby bear's porridge, chair and bed suited her as "just right."

Deeply embedded in the fairy tale is the idea of balance. The concept still drives our desires and decision-making today, doesn't it? We don't want our coffee too hot or too cold—but just right. We want our retirement portfolios balanced between conservative, moderate and aggressive asset classes. We want to achieve an appropriate balance between work and play.

The necessity for balance is everywhere, of course, and we can improve our lives by understanding how to achieve it. The next three chapters focus on physical, mental and financial balance.

CHAPTER FOUR

PHYSICAL BALANCE

"The short-term easy leads to long-term hard, and the short-term hard leads to long-term easy."

—Rory Vardin

We all know that taking care of our physical body is very important to our health and happiness. We understand that good nutrition and adequate exercise can dramatically improve our quality of life and reduce the risk that we'll develop a range of diseases and ailments.

Nevertheless, too many people lead busy, stressed-out lives that put physical balance on the back burner. This has become a problem of epic proportions in our society, and it comes with untold costs and consequences.

Plus, there's a constant blizzard of information coming at us about nutrition, exercise and overall wellness—and it seems that the "rules" often change as new studies come out. Wading through all the latest health guidance can be stressful in and of itself.

My aim in this chapter is to provide a path forward to better health through knowledge and motivation. We've all heard the adage, "If you feel good, you look good." Naturally, it's a little more complicated than that, but there are plenty of insights and strategies that we can employ in taking care of one of our most valuable possessions—our physical health.

If we think in terms of our bodies being an asset, then we must protect the thing that can make help us make our greatest contribution to the world. In Stephen R. Covey's famous book *The 7 Habits of Highly Effective People*, one of the habits—the seventh one, "sharpen the saw"—is said to be essential to the other six because it was the "principle of balanced renewal" habit that made all the others possible.

The cost of our neglect

We hear a lot these days about a supposed crisis in our health care system. There certainly are problems in that system, but I also think a former candidate for president was onto something when he said, in essence, "We don't have a health *care* crisis as much as we have a *health* crisis."

There's undoubtedly some truth to the idea that whatever problems we may have in the health system, many of them were caused by the poor choices that people make. I won't delve into all the statistics here—you've seen them in the news. But the numbers certainly substantiate the claim that we have a national crisis with respect to diabetes, heart disease and a range of other very dangerous physical conditions.

When we neglect our physical well-being, we run the risk of these conditions becoming chronic and painful. And when it hurts to move, people tend to stop moving. The maladies become harder to manage, and they overwhelm us to the point that they negatively impact our ability to function in daily life. The resulting pain, stress and anxiety can lead to even more problems, such as depression.

The amount of suffering that individuals and families have to endure because of poor health is enormous. But there also are economic costs. According to the Centers for Disease Control and Prevention, "90% of the nation's $3.8 trillion in annual health care expenditures are for people with chronic mental and health conditions." Of course, not *all* of that money could be saved if we had better health habits—but a lot of it could be.

Body, mind, spirit

Let's establish a foundation by thinking for a moment about how we were designed by our Creator. Three major components of our design pertain to what we know as *body, mind* and *spirit*. The mind and spirit are of course distinct from our physical nature, but if we ignore the connections, we're asking for trouble.

Perhaps you've encountered this quotation that's attributed to Plato: "In order for man to succeed in life, God provided him with two means, education and physical activity. Not separately, one for the soul and the other for the body, but for the two together. With these means, man can attain perfection."

Some of us may not think it's possible, in a theological sense, to attain true *perfection*, but I think Plato was wise in recognizing the value of physical activity for good health.

More to my liking is the Christian idea that our body is the temple of the Holy Spirit. That concept has profound and wide-ranging implications. But the focus of this chapter is on the question, *Is your temple in need of some maintenance?*

The physical benefits of exercise

Those of us who want to look better, feel better and be healthier have to be attentive to several factors. But there's no denying that physical exercise is right there at the center of the equation.

The Centers for Disease Control and Prevention put a sharp

focus on the matter when they wrote: "Regular physical activity helps improve your overall health, fitness, and quality of life. It also helps reduce your risk of chronic conditions like type 2 diabetes, heart disease, many types of cancer, depression and anxiety, and dementia."

Many people recognize the value of regular exercise. It makes them feel better about themselves and their appearance, and it also boosts their confidence. If you exercise today, you are more than twice as likely to feel physically attractive tomorrow.

People who exercise just a few days a week are significantly less stressed than those who do not. And then moderately strenuous exercise for about 30 minutes a day can lead to enormous benefits in terms of your mood, health, weight and ability to live an independent and fulfilling life.

Exercise doesn't need to be demanding or require super athleticism. Studies have shown that simply walking at a brisk pace for 30 minutes or more on most days can lead to significant health improvements. If you add simple strength-training exercises two or three times a week, the benefits are even greater.

Staff at the highly regarded Mayo Clinic say that even chronic conditions often can be relieved through aerobic exercise, strength training and flexibility exercises. For example, exercise can give a major boost to people afflicted with:

- *heart disease ("For people with high blood pressure, exercise can lower your risk of dying of heart disease and lower the risk of heart disease progressing.")*
- *diabetes ("Regular exercise can help insulin more effectively lower your blood sugar level.")*
- *asthma ("Often, exercise can help control the frequency and severity of asthma attacks.")*
- *back pain (Exercise and low-impact aerobics can reduce symptoms and improve muscle function.)*

- *arthritis (Exercise can "improve physical function and quality of life for people who have arthritis.")*
- *cancer (Exercise can improve quality of life for cancer patients as well as reduce the risk of dying from certain kinds of cancer.)*
- *dementia (Regular activity reduces the risk of cognitive impairment and also helps people with dementia do better.)*

What's not to like about those tremendous benefits of even moderate exercise? Just keep in mind—as the medical profession always cautions us—that we probably shouldn't attempt to go out and run a marathon (or embark on any other new exercise regimen) without consulting a doctor.

The mental benefits of exercise

Everyone knows that a workout improves our physical condition. But did you know that physical activity is good for our minds as well?

I've enjoyed following the work of Dr. John J. Ratey, who teaches psychiatry at Harvard Medical School and is recognized as "one of the world's foremost authorities on the brain-fitness connection." Perhaps you've seen him in national magazines or on the major television networks.

In recent years, Dr. Ratey has helped illuminate how physical exercise can have powerful effects on the functions of our minds. His 2008 book entitled *Spark* had a subtitle that explained exactly where his line of argument was leading: "The Revolutionary New Science of Exercise and the Brain."

As Dr. Ratey probed the connections between exercise and the mind, he found linkages in a broad array of areas. If you take even a glance at his well-known book's table of contents, you'll see that exercise can have a positive impact on conditions that plague many people—stress, anxiety, depression, addiction and aging. (Of course, that last one affects all of us in equal measure!)

As I read Dr. Ratey's book, a couple things jumped out at me, and I'd like to highlight them here. First, physical exercise accelerates learning.

When you exercise, your body releases a protein called "brain-derived neurotrophic factor" (BDNF) into the bloodstream and up to the brain. In the 1990s, scientists discovered BDNF rapidly accelerates brain-cell growth and increases one's ability to learn.

Researchers found that if they sprinkled BDNF on neurons in a petri dish, the cells automatically sprouted new branches, producing the same structural growth required for learning. BDNF gathers in reserve pools near the synapses and is unleashed when we get our blood pumping. Basically, exercise sparks the master molecule of the learning process. Dr. Ratey suggests that BDNF is kind of like "Miracle-Gro for the brain."

And then another mental benefit of physical exercise is that it enhances creativity. During exercise, the hippocampus region of the brain receives a large amount of BDNF growth factor. The hippocampus acts like a cartographer for the brain—linking new information to existing memories. A memory, scientists believe, is a collection of information fragments dispersed throughout the brain. The hippocampus serves as a way station, receiving the fragments from the cortex and then bundling them together and sending them back up as a map of a unique new pattern of connections.

Dr. Ratey also explains how exercise sparks growth in the hippocampus, helping us create new connections between existing ideas and allowing us to come up with novel solutions to complex problems. This means that if we have an important afternoon brainstorming session scheduled, it might be a smart idea to go for a short, intense run during lunch time.

Finally, I want to highlight one more positive aspect of exercise: its effect on our mental health. This may be the most important effect of all, especially during times of immense anxiety and stress of the kind that we experience during, say, a global pandemic.

Again, the staff at the Mayo Clinic give us a sense of the big picture in regard to this issue. For one thing, they say, exercise can temporarily take our minds off our worries so we can "get away from the cycle of negative thoughts that feed depression and anxiety."

But on a more physiological level, exercise releases "feel- good endorphins" that can improve the way we feel.

The bottom line, according to the Mayo Clinic, is that "working out and other forms of physical activity can definitely ease symptoms of depression or anxiety and make you feel better. Exercise may also help keep depression and anxiety from coming back once you're feeling better."

I don't believe that exercise is a panacea for every single thing that negatively affects our mental well-being—some problems can't be alleviated that easily. But it's hard to argue against the persuasive evidence that exercise is good for our mental health. We all should be committed to doing whatever our bodies permit us to do.

Be a slave to good habits

We're all slaves to our habits. It makes a lot of sense to establish good habits and then be scrupulous about adhering to them.

I'll always be grateful to the Southwestern Company for my summer job selling Bibles when I was in college—an experience that changed my perspective on how to start each day.

What I learned back then helped me develop some very positive habits that have stood the test of time. One of them is getting up early and spending some time in reading, prayer and deep contemplation. This is such a firmly entrenched part of my life that I no longer have to employ a lot of discipline to roll out of bed and get started. (The promise of a couple cups of coffee helps!)

I also have some other good habits pertaining to things like physical exercise and goal- setting. I've been doing some of these things for so long that I'm really kind of a slave to them. It's hard to imagine giving them up.

That's all on the positive side of the ledger. I'm less proud of some of my bad habits. It's part of the human condition that we'll always have to fight being a slave to things that are counterproductive in our lives. As it says in the Bible, "No one can serve two masters" (Matthew 6:24, NIV). Speaking from experience, I can confirm that this is true.

I strive really, really hard to be a physically healthy person. That's what this whole chapter is about—physical balance. Yet sometimes a bad habit can climb up out of the swamp and cause trouble. For example, I have a habit of grabbing a bite to eat in the middle of the night. I wake up and wander into the kitchen, where my weakness for sweets takes center stage. Maybe I'll have a piece of cake, a cookie, a bowl of ice cream—or the snack I like the most, peanut butter.

All the while, I'll be thinking to myself, "This isn't good for me. Why do I consume all these calories and then have to run and exercise them off in the morning?"

Like clockwork, I'll wake up the next morning and (usually!) head out for a run. It's as if my demon of 2 a.m. snacks never made an appearance.

I believe this kind of daily decision-making is reality for most of us at some level. We're always making choices, and the ones we make—even the small ones—end up becoming habits and revealing what it is that we're serving. That's why it's so important to be mindful of the kinds of habits we develop and embrace. If we're going to be slaves to habits, let's make them good ones.

The investment perspective on habits

During my 40 years of helping clients prepare for and deal with life's uncertainties, I've had to consult with them on issues relating to financial balance and their monetary investments. (We'll spend chapter 6 exploring the financial angle.)

But I also like to use the investment perspective when thinking about the habits connected to physical health. If we think about it for a moment, we'll probably realize that the health habits we develop are a lot like investments.

If we invest in bad health habits, eventually they will cost us dearly—just like a bad investment in the stock market can wreck a retirement account. Conversely, good health habits will dramatically improve our chances of living a longer, healthier life. That's a wise investment in my book.

Now, it requires an effort to consciously invest in good health choices. The reason: Neuroscience research has revealed that only about 5% of the decisions we make daily are the result of our conscious mind at work. This means that 95% of what we do is governed by our *unconscious* mind.

Have you ever driven home from work and realized that you can't remember a single moment of the journey? You made a lot of decisions—about stopping at a light and turning into your neighborhood. But they didn't really register. That's the unconscious mind at work. It's similar to breathing, picking up your foot to take a step or sipping from a coffee cup. Much of what we do isn't really the result of conscious choice.

You can see how this applies to the decisions we make—consciously or unconsciously—about our physical health. To reiterate a point we discussed earlier, we really are a slave to our habits. That's why it can be so difficult for us to get in the rhythm of new and healthier choices. If we can think about it this way, what we really need to do is break the habit of being ourselves. That sounds like a daunting task, doesn't it?

Consciously setting goals can help, and we'll talk about that a bit later in this chapter. But we may also need to work on "reprogramming" our subconscious minds.

Try to think about your mind in terms of an old-fashioned tape recorder. As you live your life, your patterns constitute a kind of recording that plays over and over again. The tape is almost like the soundtrack of your life.

In order to change the recording (or perhaps "the narrative" in modern parlance), we need to record new information over the old, counterproductive stuff. For example, if we've developed bad health habits, we need to invest in our body by recording over those bad habits with positive ones.

Changing our habits and acquiring a new way of operating will undoubtedly require a lot of time, energy and concentration. But before long, the new behaviors will become normal—which of course means that we'll have new habits. The investment will increase our happiness, productivity and effectiveness, which in turn will yield the improved physical balance that this chapter is all about.

Keep your body hydrated

The importance of physical exercise has been highlighted in this chapter, but there are some other very important and often-neglected aspects of physical balance—such as the need to supply your body with enough water for optimum performance. The consequences of depriving your body of sufficient water can be truly negative.

Water is essential to body functions that involve thermoregulation, cognition and the gastrointestinal, kidney and circulatory systems. If you don't get enough water, you can suffer headaches—and much worse.

Without a doubt, water is a vital nutrient. I'm sure you've heard it before: You can live for weeks, maybe months, without food—but you'll survive less than a week without water.

How do you determine if you're drinking enough water? For one thing, if you're thirsty, you're already dehydrated. Additionally, there's the age-old method of checking the color of your urine. The lighter the color, the more hydrated you are.

Minor dehydration—which can cause problems with all of the previously mentioned systems and functions—can be addressed simply by replenishing your body with its missing fluids. But you don't want to let minor dehydration become a major problem. If you take only one thing out of this chapter, let it be this: Drink plenty of water.

Here's an action step to get you started. Drink a big bottle of water three times a day—morning, noon and early evening. I've used this system, and I guarantee that it will change your body, mind and spirit for the better. In the words of the famous 1970s commercial for Alka- Seltzer, "Try it—you'll like it."

Get enough rest

Any number of reports indicate that sleep deprivation has become an epidemic in our society. I suspect that some of the problem is caused by social media. Many people simply have difficulty turning off the cellphone and going to sleep at night. There's always one more link to click or one more social-media message to read. Consequently, people stay awake later than they should, and they don't get the rest they need to recharge their body.

The amount of sleep we need changes as we age. For example, according to the CDC, schoolchildren should have nine to 12 hours of sleep per day, while adults 65 and older need only seven to eight hours. But millions of people simply don't get enough sleep. The CDC reports that more than a third of adults get less than seven hours a night.

The clear consequence of sleep deprivation is that our minds and bodies won't function as well as they should. In fact, serious health risks are associated with insufficient sleep.

A publication from Johns Hopkins reviews some very sobering numbers. Sleep deprivation gives us a 33% increase in the risk of dementia, a 48% increase in the risk of heart disease, and—if we get less than five hours of sleep per night—a 50% increase in the risk of obesity. We'll also increase our risk of high blood pressure and have a three-times-higher risk of developing type 2 diabetes. In addition, we'll be at greater risk of depression, irritability, anxiety, forgetfulness and "fuzzy thinking."

Interestingly, the CDC reports that being awake for 18 hours is akin to having a blood alcohol content of .05%. Even worse, staying awake for 24 hours is equivalent to having a blood alcohol level of .10%, which is higher than the legal limit in all 50 states.

How can you improve the quality of your rest and thus your health? The American Academy of Sleep Medicine offers a number of tips. A few of my favorites are:

- *maintaining a consistent sleep schedule*
- *exercising daily*
- *eating a well-balanced diet*
- *avoiding large meals before bedtime*
- *turning off electronic devices at least 30 minutes before bedtime*

All of those tips are important, but don't neglect the focus of this chapter—exercise. I have a client who swears that her sleep quality is much better when she walks several miles during the day.

It can take some time to establish better sleep habits and begin to feel the benefits. And of course if you suffer from a sleep condition such as apnea, managing your sleep may be more difficult.

But there are still important steps that we all can take to improve our sleep. In large part, it's a matter of breaking out of bad habits and introducing better, healthier ones.

In chapter 3, we learned how to become more aware of what's important in life. It follows that one of our highest priorities should be—sorry about this!—to *learn how to prioritize*. This applies to sleep. If we underinvest in getting the rest our body needs, we devalue the asset that makes all our other achievements possible. Sleep allows us to operate at our highest level of performance and achieve more in less time. If you want to have a competitive advantage in your body, mind and spirit, get your rest and protect your most valuable asset.

Choices and goals

It's a lot easier to keep making bad choices than it is to make good ones, at least at first. And sometimes we might have perfectly legitimate reasons for not taking care of ourselves the way we should. We're mindful of the fact that some people have physical conditions or injuries that simply make it impossible for them to engage in the kind of physical exercise we've been discussing, or they have other kinds of limitations that don't allow them to follow some of the best practices that we're encountering in this chapter.

Often, however, an excuse is just that—an excuse. And I want to suggest that we can harness the power of choices and the technique of goal-setting that we discussed in chapter three to get off the proverbial couch and make some real progress.

We live in a data-driven society, and even though we won't need to hire a software engineer from Silicon Valley to analyze the numbers, we might be able to generate some very simple data that connects to our personal choices and goals.

For example, we should ask what needs to change in order for our physical health to improve. Do we drink too much, smoke or eat junk food too many times a week? Do we suffer from chronic pain or health conditions because we don't take enough breaks to stretch our muscles when working at a desk? Do we give in to the temptation to binge-watch television all evening rather than take a walk?

Each one of these situations has aspects that can be measured and monitored—data, in other words. I suggest starting by taking inventory. If diet is a concern, we can download a food- tracking app and log what we eat for a week before we begin to make changes.

If we worry about a sedentary lifestyle, we can track our activity with a fitness watch or the app on a smartphone. Smoking? Count the cigarettes. Drinking? Count the liquid ounces. Sleep? A fitness watch can tell you exactly how much rest you get every night.

This first stage is all about awareness. We pay attention. We make ourselves aware of the rhythms of our life. When we see the data on a phone or computer screen, we'll be more ready than ever to take the next steps. We have to know where we're starting from in order to move ahead.

Once we know what the baseline is, we move on to the next stage. With solid information from our family doctor or specialist, as well as what we've learned in our own research, we establish some realistic goals. If necessary, go back to chapter three for a refresher course in how to brainstorm and set quantifiable goals.

Goals will of course vary from person to person depending on individual circumstances, but it won't be hard to figure out what your targets might be. For example, people who have neglected their health for years may need to start with modest expectations. I'm not dispensing medical advice here—consult with your doctor. But it wouldn't be unusual for someone to set a goal of building up to a 30-minute walk every other day.

In my situation, I might set a preliminary goal of cutting in half the amount of food I consume during my midnight raids of the kitchen. (That would be a very good start indeed.) Or I might set a goal over the next year of increasing the miles I run by 5%.

When it comes to something like smoking, the goal would be easy and obvious: slam on the brakes and get down to zero cigarettes.

As we pursue our fitness goals, we don't stop collecting data. We continue logging our activity so that we can better discern the rhythms of our life and the progress that we're making.

If we see the bar chart moving downward on the weight-loss scale, it will encourage us to stay the course.

I believe in baby steps, so I recommend starting with modest expectations and goals. Forward progress is what it takes. We just have to start moving in the right direction.

If we're overly ambitious, chances are that we'll experience some degree of failure and quit in discouragement. But if we start small, we'll be able to stack success on top of success. Eventually, we'll be in a position to take longer strides.

The index-card approach to goals

We have so much to gain and so little to lose when we take care of our bodies. But it all starts with commitment—and solidifying that commitment can be boosted with (once again) the humble but powerful 3x5 card.

Here's how it works. First, identify a habit or trait that you'd like to change, and write it down on a card. For example, maybe you'd like to get off the couch and be more active by taking walks or riding a bike.

Next, take out a second card and write down all the benefits you'd expect to see if you were to implement that change. In our example, you'd expect to see better physical health, you'd feel less lethargic, you'd have an improved frame of mind, you'd feel better about yourself, etc. It's been said that if you give yourself enough reasons for why doing something is important, you can do almost anything—so that's what we're working on here.

Step three on the third card: Write down three things you must do to achieve the goal.

The fourth step and card involve writing down three positive steps you'll take *this week* to move you toward your goal.

Finally, on the fifth card, write down three things that could stop you from accomplishing your goal—and use this as a warning and mechanism for not letting them get in your way.

Read your collection of cards three times a day—morning, noon and night—to keep your goal at the forefront of your mind. It might take three days just to get the bugs worked out, but after three weeks you'll have formed a new habit—and after three months, the positive change will be programmed into your subconscious mind. This technique works for me, and if you give it a shot, I think it'll work for you as well.

Forming a good habit works exactly the same as forming a bad habit. Which type of habit do you prefer?

The right rhythms

This chapter is illuminating various factors that help us maintain our sense of balance with respect to physical health. We're seeing that we need adequate sleep, sufficient hydration, a good diet and more time spent moving—but making all this happen seems like a daunting task.

Honestly, if we score poorly on these factors, it'll probably take a total life transformation to make the kinds of changes that put us on the road to physical balance—and change can be a tough enemy to defeat because we humans tend to be lazy and stubborn. We get comfortable in our daily rhythms and habits.

We need to take inventory from time to time and see what rhythms have wrapped their bony fingers around our schedules, our cravings and our workouts to the point where our well-being suffers. We want to be aware of how our life rhythms end up promoting—or undermining—our good health.

When it comes to the rhythms in my own life, I want them to amount to be a resounding song of worship for my Creator. I believe

He has made us all to be vessels that will fill up and spill over with goodness—and that includes physical wellness.

I want to take care of my physical body because this home is the only one I have—there's no replacing this vital part of me. There is no replacing yours, either. This home, this temple, is the only one we get on this planet—and once it's all used up, it's gone. Yes, our bodies are going to deteriorate as we get older; there's no way to completely stop that natural process. But if we take care of them well, they won't have to break down so soon, and we can live more healthful and fulfilling lives for a longer period of time.

Making exercise happen

We all agree that exercise is critically important to our physical balance, so what's the reason so many people skip the workouts? (No, getting off the couch to grab some more potato chips doesn't qualify as a vigorous walk!)

One reason is that we often prefer to seek short-term rewards rather than long-term benefits. The so-called "Esau Syndrome"—based on the biblical story of the famished elder brother who sold his birthright for a bowl of stew—probably can be applied to the exercise habits (or lack thereof) that many people have. It's just a lot easier to cash in on that perceived short-term benefit (another tasty bowl of ice cream) than it is to pay the price for long-term health by doing something difficult and uncomfortable (working out).

Another factor working against regular life-giving exercise is that we might have become too soft among all the physical comforts we have. Some people keep the home thermostat set at a comfortable 72 degrees all year long. We sleep on mattresses that allow us to set the degree of firmness. I plead guilty to owning a car that gives me the luxury of heated seats, a heated steering wheel, windows that automatically melt off the snow and ice—and even the ability to play therapeutic Rolling Stones classics over a Bose sound system.

I've wondered if all this pampering ends up training us to be intolerant of the kind of discomfort that comes from doing a demanding workout.

And of course we have plenty of excuses at our disposal when we don't want to hit the weights or lace up the running shoes. "I don't want to get sweaty." "I hate it when my hair gets messed up." "It's too hot (or cold) out there." "I just don't have the time."

I challenge you to look your excuse(s) in the eye and use the power of three to get things going:

- *Try it for three days.*
- *It takes only three weeks to form a habit.*
- *It takes only three months to reprogram your subconscious mind.*

And here are three techniques that can be helpful:

- *Simplify your workout regimen.* Abandon the all-or- nothing myth. Develop a cycle of making and keeping small commitments that build into more-ambitious changes.
- *Expand your horizon.* Dispense with any narrow-minded attitudes you've had about exercise. Instead, concentrate on your energy levels, do more things you love, and make becoming healthy a side effect of your lifestyle.
- *Experiment.* Try new approaches that might work better for you. If one workout regimen, such as running, doesn't motivate you, try something else, such as biking or swimming. It might even be helpful or necessary to find a personal trainer who can help devise a personalized exercise plan that's more enjoyable.

Overcoming the challenge of motivation

By now, the value of exercise is abundantly clear. We all know we should exercise. There are tons of benefits.

But why is it so difficult to get going sometimes? According to a recent report from the CDC, less than a quarter of American adults—22.9%—met the recommended guidelines for both aerobic and muscle-strengthening activities during what they call "leisure-time physical activity."

That leaves 77.1% of our fellow citizens not getting the exercise they need—nor the physical, emotional, mental and spiritual benefits that accrue from being active.

Naturally, much of the problem can be attributed to lack of motivation. To overcome that, we need something called "initiation energy." That's really just a fancy way of saying that we need to break through the imaginary mental force that holds so many of us back from doing what we know we should do. Imagine you're a  rocket ship trying to break the earth's gravity—it takes tons of power at first, and then later it's a lot easier to travel though outer space.

My plastic tub of index cards contains this relevant quote from the motivational speaker Tony Robbins: "It's been said that there are only two pains in life, the pain of discipline or the pain of regret, and discipline weighs ounces while regret weighs tons."

Discipline comes into play in hundreds of moments in our daily lives when we make these seemingly small but eventually very significant decisions. When we make positive choices, they can improve our mood (and much more) for the rest of the day. And in the long run, they can reduce our chances of getting ill from various diseases and ailments.

In contrast, when we make poor choices, they decrease our energy for the rest of the day and over the years increase the likelihood of chronic problems.

One choice we have is to live by our feelings, emotions and impulses, which typically could have us give in to the easy way—and have us spend the entire evening in "couch-potato mode." Or we can choose to let our actions be governed by reason, logic and rational thinking, which would push us in the direction of getting up and engaging in some physical activity—which we know would be better for us in the long run.

When we encounter that moment of truth and have to make a decision about taking it easy or getting our blood pumping, we can use the power of three to make the right call: *pause, think* and *react.* The pausing and thinking process can help us focus on short- and long-term benefits of physical exercise, making it more likely that we do the right thing. But if we only react, we might end up staying on that oh-so-comfortable couch.

It must be said that motivation is easy to come by at times—such as when we make New Year's resolutions. But it's much harder to stick with the program over the long haul. If we miss a couple days in our new exercise regimen, it's easy to become discouraged and never get back to it.

I think we can address this problem through a practice called *kaizen*, which is Japanese for a concept that could be described as "continuous improvement." A lot of companies use this model to increase quality and productivity over time.

Perhaps that perspective can help us make progress as we seek to improve our physical health. The key is to understand that we don't have to make revolutionary changes overnight. We aren't likely to succeed if we set the bar too high—by doing a daily triathlon, for example.

But if we at least can make small, incremental changes in our habits, we can reap tremendous benefits over time. And before long, some of the most dedicated practitioners of this approach might actually find themselves doing that triathlon.

What if I don't have the time to exercise?

An excellent book entitled *The One Minute Workout* is based on the premise that you can get all the exercise you need in just three minutes of hard exercise per week. If you don't believe me, read the book and review the scientific research presented there. The author, Martin Gibala, Ph.D., shows how very short, intense bursts of exercise are the most potent workout available. The health-promoting value of this so-called HIIT ("high intensity interval training") system for preventing and reversing disease is amazing. And the beauty of it is that you can get the job done in one minute.

Don't do this without your doctor's permission, but next time you have a chance, run through 30 burpees as fast as you can. (Not sure what a burpee is? Google it.)

Note how long the set takes—it shouldn't be much more than a minute. But if we do that only three times a week, we'll boost our endurance, increase our metabolism, regulate our insulin levels and lose body fat. The more intensely we do the exercise, the more calories we'll burn.

Now, imagine sprinting to save a child from an oncoming car. That experience would shock your system into producing the different chemicals you need to perform the rescue. That's kind of how burpees work in terms of attaining the benefits you want from exercise. The good news is that the pain is over in 30 seconds, and you need to have only three blasts, three times a week, to equal 150 minutes of regular exercise. We can get this effect in various ways, including bicycling, sprinting and doing burpees—as long as the bursts are intense. No special location, no special equipment and no gym membership are needed. Try it for three days, and you'll be amazed. In three weeks, you'll be changed, and in three months, you'll be transformed.

Moving forward with determination

We can read all the motivational and self-help books we want, but in the final analysis, only we as individuals can change our lives. That's where the power and the impetus for change reside.

It's obvious that we need to take care of ourselves. But when we find ourselves immersed in the stresses, anxieties and pressures of daily life, it can take a small miracle for us to even remember that something called self-compassion exists.

Nevertheless, our physical balance is so important that we have to *fight* for our well-being. In all likelihood, that may mean making certain sacrifices. But as we saw earlier in this chapter, it doesn't have to take a lot of time to do the kind of high- intensity workout that can have a major impact on our health. With a modicum of discipline, we can make our lives not just livable but lovable. We can thrive in life—but first, we have to be willing to move.

CHAPTER FIVE

MENTAL BALANCE

*"The most important story you will ever tell
about yourself is the story you tell **to** yourself."*
— *Jim Loehr*

Our last chapter focused on physical health—which, as we saw, is essential to successful living. But we have to keep more than one plate spinning in our lives. Although taking care of our bodies is important, we can't afford to neglect our *mental* health.

Far too many people seem to think that as long as they're not depressed or overly anxious, they're "about as good as it gets" with respect to their mental balance. But that certainly doesn't mean that they're really hitting on all cylinders—they probably can do much better. This chapter offers a plan for optimizing our sense of emotional and mental well-being.

By the way, instead of using the term mental health, I generally prefer to speak of *mental balance* and *emotional balance*—depending on the context. That's the nomenclature you'll often see in the following pages.

Now, before we get too far into this chapter, I urge you to pause and contemplate what condition you're in mentally. Take a self-inventory. Think about your emotional state. Ask if there are difficult experiences in your life that you may still need to resolve. Consider whether you devote enough time to taking care of yourself emotionally. Are there aspects of your mental balance that you could improve through self-compassion, counseling or community building?

If you're struggling, there are many resources designed to help. Don't be afraid to seek them out. Whatever stigma that used to be associated with mental challenges is dissipating, so there's every reason to choose the path of wellness.

We can't afford to neglect our mental balance. It needs to be a priority.

A formative experience with reading

Who among us hasn't had a bad school experience—or even a *very* bad one? I absolutely, positively had one of the latter when I was in elementary school. I'm going to begin this chapter with that sad tale because it sets up our discussion of mental balance. (But don't worry—the "sad tale" has a very happy ending.)

When I was in elementary school in the 1960s, my teacher used a reading system designed by Science Research Associates, Inc. I'm sure this color-coded reading program was intended to help kids read. But in my case, it turned into a brick wall and major discouragement.

Each color in the SRA system represented a level of reading comprehension. Unfortunately for me, I never made it past level one—the "red" color. I simply could not advance. Reading didn't seem to be my gift.

I'll never forget the heartache I felt each time my teacher would look down at me and say, "I think you need to stay put." Then, with her next breath, she'd congratulate classmates for their abilities. Oh, how I longed to be in the blue and aqua color levels of the smart kids!

My reading skills never did improve throughout elementary

school, and by fourth grade, I had to be held back. My parents were understandably concerned, so they took me to a counselor.

It turned out that my eyes were not tracking properly. They darted about on the pages crammed with words and letters, making comprehension nearly impossible. There was nothing they could do.

When an elementary student's self-esteem has been wrecked, the climb back to mental balance is no easy task. And since my teachers didn't seem to think I had much academic potential, I decided early on that I'd never be a serious student. There was only one other role or identity that seemed within my reach. I became a troublemaker.

By middle school, I was being paddled and disciplined all the time. High school was a blur of smoking pot, taking illegal drugs and drinking lots of beer, vodka and whiskey. I skipped school and partied on weekends. I wore a t-shirt that displayed what had become my unofficial motto: "Sworn to fun, loyal to none."

I graduated from high school as part of the 1976 bicentennial class, but I ranked in the bottom 10%. The guidance counselor gave me a brochure on the Army and an application to a glass factory that was hiring for the summer. No college viewbooks for me!

But that wasn't the end of the story

Finally, my dad had seen enough of my devil-may-care attitude, and as a schoolteacher, he knew the value of a good education. He cornered me that summer after I graduated, and he declared that something had to change—I had to do something with my life.

I ruled out the Army when I decided I couldn't live without my ponytail, and I didn't want to do hot and sweaty work in a glass factory. College sounded fun since I was aware of the partying scene, but I figured that my grades weren't good enough to get me accepted.

Nevertheless, my dad sent off an application in my name to Ball

State University, not far from where we lived. And it turned out that my grades were exactly what Ball State was looking for.

They accepted me into an experimental academic-opportunity program, essentially so I could be a guinea pig for their education majors. They were going to teach teachers how to teach students like me to read.

Imagine my shock and horror when I showed up for a required class and learned that they were going to use the SRA color-coded reading program on me. Oh, no—not those stories and questions again! Would I ever advance out of the red level?

But soon a student in the teacher's college looked at me and said, "Steve, would you be willing to let me teach you how to speed read?"

I probably looked at her like I thought she was crazy. She was proposing *speed reading* for someone who may have been the slowest reader on campus?

By this time, I'd pretty much given up hope that I'd ever be a good reader. There wasn't much fight left in me. So without much resistance, I consented to the plan. (Also, the terms of my state-funded experimental academic program dictated that I *had* to do what they told me.)

It took a while, but eventually I learned how to speed read. More importantly, I learned how to read for *deep comprehension*. My technique involved reading with a pen in hand—underling passages, scribbling notes in the margins, and even making notes on the index cards that would later become so important to me.

Developing the ability to read—which at first seemed like an insurmountable obstacle on my educational journey—ended up changing *everything* for me. It was like a switch had flipped on.

I fell in love with reading. I'd go to the college library and pick up a book, finish it in a few days, and then try another. A couple of my favorites were Norman Vincent Peale's *The Power of Positive Thinking* and *The Tough-Minded Optimist*. I'd always read every book by my favorite authors. I even began to read and study material that wasn't assigned by my professors.

My parents got the shock of their lives when they received a letter inviting them to the induction ceremony for Alpha Lambda Delta— the freshman honor society for students with high GPAs. I still have the little pin I was given that day.

My perspective on the world shifted almost overnight when the formerly impossible task of reading became a vital, joyous gift. Since then, there have been many years in which I've read 40, 50, even 60 books—all because I just love to read.

I've always wondered if receiving this gift of reading was coincidence, luck or divine providence. Whatever it was, I'll always remain very grateful for the miracle that allowed me to graduate from college and start my life on a better path.

But the takeaway is that for more than a decade of my young life, I was saddled with the label of "slow reader and bad student." I owned that name tag. It affected my attitude and my decisions.

And of course it threw off my mental balance, which—as you can see—led me to a bad place indeed. I'm very glad I was able to recover. Now let's delve into what mental balance is and how to achieve and maintain it.

What it means to be mentally balanced

I've come to the conclusion that mentally balanced people have developed the capacity to do three things. First, they're able to understand reality. The implications of this are tremendous for every aspect of our lives, so this is where we begin.

Modern psychiatry refers to this as the reality principle— the means by which we see the world as it is and ourselves as we really are. Naturally, people can err on either side of the reality continuum. Some people—you've probably met a few—think they're incapable of doing wrong, and they hold themselves in high esteem indeed. But perhaps many more people falsely think of themselves as inferior and unworthy.

In contrast to these unhelpful extremes, a mentally balanced person has both feet planted squarely on the solid ground of reality— that being that *every person* is infinitely valuable in the eyes of our Creator. Such a person has the strength to accept grace, see the truth, and not be misled by false ideas about self-worth.

A realistic handle on reality can help us avoid the temptation to feel that we're worthless. It can help us embrace life, not run from it. It can help us avoid the trap of coping with negative feelings by withdrawing from relationships, developing addictions, and working so hard that we don't have time to think about the pain we're experiencing.

Further, mentally balanced people don't make impossible demands on themselves, don't expect to be perfect, and don't try to live up to unrealistically high standards. They don't engage in self-condemnation. They don't allow themselves to be plagued by a sense of inferiority or inadequacy. They don't constantly compete with themselves or others in a misguided effort to prove that they're worthy.

The mentally healthy person is not conceited or overly confident but does have a healthy measure of self-respect. A positive attitude towards oneself and other people is a hallmark of mental balance.

Acceptance is a key concept here. Healthy people accept the good and the bad, the happy and the sad, and all the ups and downs of life in general. They understand that they can be proactive and take responsibility—not just see themselves as victims.

In sum, a person who is mentally healthy has a firm grasp of his or her ultimate value as a person. This individual has a deep sense that life is worth the effort and that we should live with zest, purpose and spirit. This kind of approach to life is essential to mental balance.

Defeating worry

The second thing that mentally balanced people have the ability to do is be at peace with themselves and the universe. I'm not talking here about embracing some kind of new-age philosophy. I'm talking about accepting the reality of our lives without undue worrying.

Yes, life often throws us a curve ball, and sometimes it even feels like someone has whacked us over the head with the baseball bat. We all feel that sensation at some point.

But too many people spend too much of their lives haunted by the prospect of bad things that in all likelihood won't happen. Worrying about the future means that we invest a tremendous amount of our energy, strength and vitality in fighting figments of our imagination.

Worry has a corrosive effect on our ability to live the kind of life we want to lead. People who fall into the trap of excessive worrying find themselves debilitated and disempowered. A chronic state of worry is one of the principal symptoms of neurosis.

The humorist Erma Bombeck put a lighter spin on it when she wrote, "Worry is like a rocking chair: it gives you something to do but never gets you anywhere."

She understood the plain fact that worry can't solve a single problem.

In contrast, mentally balanced people don't spend a lot of time and energy anticipating the problems that *might* arise. Instead, they deal with problems only when—and if—they land on the doorstep. Such people have the ability to concentrate on today's troubles and resist the temptation to worry about what might happen tomorrow. In popular parlance, this is known as "living one day at a time."

Many readers of this book will be familiar with the so-called "serenity prayer." Consider the words:

> *God, grant me the serenity to accept the things*
> *I cannot change,*

courage to change the things I can,
and the wisdom to know the difference.

It's a simple prayer, but it encapsulates the essence of this critically important aspect of mental balance.

Ability to give and receive love

The third—and perhaps most important—characteristic of mentally balanced people is that they cultivate the ability to give and receive love.

Loving is the thing that frees us from the prison of our own existence, takes us out of ourselves, makes us a part of other people's lives, and gives meaning and purpose to our own life.

We all long to have happy, healthy, loving relationships with other human beings. The mentally balanced person finds pleasure and fulfillment in these associations. I say that such a person has faith in other people—free of chronic suspiciousness and distrust about motives.

Yes, we sometimes can be disappointed by the decisions that people make. But the healthy personality is resilient and strong enough to bear the disappointments of life—just as a healthy body is strong enough to hold up under a reasonable amount of physical strain.

Someone who is mentally balanced functions as an integral part of society, has a sense of responsibility for their fellow man, and buys into the English poet John Donne's well-known statement that "No man is an island."

This is not merely a modern insight. One of the most inspiring passages in the Bible is the so-called "love chapter," which states, in part: "And if I have the gift of prophecy, and know all mysteries and all knowledge; and if I have all faith, so as to remove mountains, but have not love, I am nothing" (1 Corinthians 13:2, ASV).

In contrast, sadly, out-of-balance people can't seem to develop loving relationships, and they're preoccupied with their own concerns.

Knowing who we are

No doubt you've seen yourself in the distorted, wavy reflection of a "funhouse mirror." Just as that kind of mirror fails to reveal what we really look like, our human nature also can lead us down a path of false identity.

It's impossible to live with a strong sense of mental balance if we don't really know who we are. Of course, I'm not talking about amnesia or whether we know our Myers-Briggs personality type. I'm referring to something much more fundamental—like whether we understand our value in the grand design of the universe.

Now, I'll get a little spiritual here as we deal with this issue. I believe we all have a personal designer and creator. We know Him as God. Above all, He loves us. He hears our cries, He knows our needs, and He wants us to reach out to Him. It's His desire that we have blessings, happiness and joy in abundance.

If we have that perspective, each one of us is named—in a manner of speaking—"You are enough." *Enough.* That means we don't have to live up to some arbitrary and superficial standard that the culture wants to impose on us.

These days, it can be hard for some to accept that they have that kind of inherent value. I'm sure that stems in part from the fact that we constantly compare ourselves to others through social media. We're probably all tempted to feel that we're not as good as other people. We look at the Facebook feeds of our friends and conclude that they're living the life—and we're not. And if they're doing better, we may be tempted to conclude that we're worth less. But of course this faulty line of thinking is one of the fundamental causes of unhappiness for people in our society.

Mental balance also requires us to avoid thinking of our value in terms of what we own or what we do for a living.

You might say, "I'm a business owner." But no—that's not who you are. That's how you earn money and put food on the table.

You might say, "I'm a golfer." No. Unless you play on the pro circuit, playing golf is just a hobby and a way to relieve stress.

Is our value as a person dependent on whether we drive a $60,000 sports car or a rusty old beater with a noisy muffler? Or whether we own a mansion on the beach or a two-bedroom ranch? Or whether we're gainfully employed or just got laid off? Or whether we maintained or lost our health?

No.

It can be hard to wrap our minds around this truth because of the materialistic culture we live in, but we're not defined by what we own, what we do for a living or what we look like. Our value has nothing to do with possessions, professions or superficial characteristics such as height, weight and color of skin, hair and eyes. In the mind of our Creator, those things have nothing to do with our value as human beings.

Instead, we are enough because God created and loves us. We should strive to focus not on what differentiates us but on what we have in common—such as the desire to belong to a group, enjoy satisfying relationships, have meaningful work, and make ourselves and the world around us better.

Remember that when we see our Creator for who He really is, we become a "new creature" (2 Corinthians 5:17, KJV). The Spirit does not come into our lives to patch up our current identity but to give us a new identity as a redeemed child of God. Our feelings of inferiority, insecurity and inadequacy are exchanged for a peace that surpasses all understanding and comprehension.

If we can grasp the truth that "My name is enough," we'll be able to restore the kind of mental balance that we were designed to live with.

The stories we tell ourselves

Years ago when I started paying attention to how the mind works, I thought positive thinking was the answer. All I needed to do, I figured, was think positive, and everything would work out just fine.

Well, positive thinking is of course much better than negative thinking. It can help us recognize what's good in our lives, and it can be a buffer against many mental disorders. There are dots to be connected here with our previous chapter on gratitude.

But there's more to it than merely positive thinking. We need to take that a step farther and focus more specifically on the "stories we tell ourselves."

Ever since movies were introduced back around the turn of the 20th century, they've been one of the great storytelling mediums. Of course, not everything that comes out of Hollywood has deep, life-changing significance—to say the least! But movies do have the potential to change the way we see things and have a lasting impact on our lives.

The key thing is the *story*. That's what makes a film great. You can have talented actors, a wonderful soundtrack and excellent cinematography, but if the story isn't compelling, a movie won't... move us.

Now, if the quality of a story plays such a central role in the value of an evening's entertainment, think of how much more important our life stories are. What are the stories we tell ourselves about our purpose, our value, our trajectories through eternal time?

When you think about it in these terms, our lives are stories, and we're the scriptwriter, the producer, the director, the lead actor, the set designer, the special-effects coordinator—even the audience. And if we don't like the way the story arc is going, we can try to change it.

As we think about how we write our stories, it can be helpful to keep three things in mind. First, *anything is possible*. In any given situation, there may be more possibilities than we imagine. What is possible becomes the fuel of potential. Too often, people limit themselves because they don't keep their minds open to all possible outcomes and courses of action. Our existence becomes like a car stuck in first gear. The engine is revving up and working hard, but the vehicle will be extremely limited in how far and fast it can go. It really comes down to expanding our belief system to its full potential.

Secondly, *we have the power to choose.* The theological concept of "free will" teaches us that we have the innate ability to choose our thoughts, feelings and actions. Unfortunately, this can be a blind spot for many people. Too many get into the habit of behaviors and beliefs that lead to complacence and stagnation. We live in a world of excuse-makers, blamers and people who simply refuse to be accountable for their circumstances. We will never achieve mental balance unless we embrace our freedom to choose. In an often-used formula, it just takes patience, practice and persistence.

Thirdly, *we need to obey the law of authenticity.* Mental balance and fulfillment in life are possible only if we're in full harmony with ourselves. The phrase "be true to yourself" applies here. It simply doesn't work to try to become someone or something that we're not. We won't be happier if we behave in a certain way, acquire certain possessions, or earn more money. The truth is that to be at our happiest and most fulfilled, we need to be more aware of and embrace our individuality, uniqueness and purpose.

These are all essential components of our life story. Remember, if we aren't focused on thoughtfully writing our own story, our mental and emotional balance will suffer.

Self-compassion and mental balance

Like everything else that's worthwhile in life, achieving mental balance requires some effort. How do we make a habit of adequately maintaining our equilibrium? It all begins with self-compassion.

We've probably all heard variations of the phrase "you can't draw water from an empty well" over the years, and the statement has sticking power because it expresses a fundamental truth. When we're worn down, emptied out and overspent, there's nothing left for us to give.

Some of our individual choices don't exactly help promote strong mental balance. For example, it's not rejuvenating for us to continuously scroll through our Facebook feeds, fire off angry tweets, and obsess over how many likes we get for an Instagram photo. The algorithms crafted by Silicon Valley engineers have succeeded in getting and keeping us addicted. Many people have a hard time turning off the smartphone even when they fall dead-tired into bed.

When we combine this phenomenon of technology and social media with the ordinary pressures of our busy lives, we find that we may not do a good job taking care of ourselves. The well runs dry. We neglect our mental balance.

How can we get a handle on this all-too-common situation and ramp up our level of self-compassion?

I think it's essential to figure out what's draining the battery juice. When we reach the end of a particularly long or hard day or week, it's good to take inventory. What were the things that had the greatest negative impact—either at work or at home? What brought us down? What would we most like to change?

The problem might be work worries, family drama, financial unease or other sources of stress. It certainly isn't possible to eliminate every stressor, or probably even most of them, from our lives—not in this world, at least. But if we can take a clear-eyed look at where the turbulence is in our lives, maybe that can help us open up even a little bit of space for self-compassion and rejuvenation.

And then what does that self-compassion look like? It works differently for everyone, but here are a few simple techniques or strategies that I'd suggest.

First, turn off the spigot of distraction from the aforementioned social media. It seems fairly obvious that we can't really manage relationships and be productive in our work when our email and social media are constantly demanding our attention. Beep, beep, beep—the notifications can go on all day, interrupting our concentration and causing us to miss important moments with family and friends. If we're at the family dinner table or out with friends, and we don't have the ability to put the phone away—that's a danger sign.

Another good piece of advice is to plug the phone in for overnight charging in the kitchen, office or family room—not in the bedroom where we sleep. Why? If the phone is in the bedroom, we likely won't be able to resist letting it keep us up late at night—and we'll make checking it the first thing we do in the morning. These behaviors are not conducive to mental balance.

I've heard it said that "If you have a smartphone, you have a smartphone addiction." That may not be true in every case, but I think there's something to the general idea. That makes it necessary for those of us who are smartphone users to "unplug" for a while, even during the day. If I find myself getting too stressed or overwhelmed, I shut off my phone and head for a park or hiking trail. You may prefer to take a bike ride or write in a journal.

But the point is that we need to clean out the muck that builds up in our heads over time. We need time to ourselves in order to think through big decisions and stay focused on what's most important. The longer we stay distracted, the harder it becomes to break free of the cycle and actually work through what's happening in our lives.

Processing emotions

That brings us to the important task of learning how to process emotions as a strategy for self-compassion. We'd never want to deny the role of emotions, whether positive or negative, in our lives. But we do need to process them in a constructive way and—if necessary—move on.

My suggestion is that we build some time into our schedules for thinking through our emotions. This is a vital part of maintaining mental health, and it should be done on a regular basis. In fact, it should become a habit. We can write it down on our schedules or set a recurring reminder on our phones. Label the appointment "Self-compassion, because I'm worth it."

Adequate processing requires that we cognitively understand what has happened, that we work through our emotional responses, and that we can learn from what we've experienced. Of course, some events and circumstances can't be processed all at once but rather must be undertaken as a journey. For serious traumas or emotional stressors, it's important to find a therapist whom we can trust and who can help us deal with situations fruitfully.

The point, however, is that it's difficult to achieve a state of mental balance if we don't develop the capacity to productively deal with the emotions we feel.

What cancer taught me about balance

Our emotional balance can take a real shellacking from time to time when a crisis hits us over the head with a 2-by-4. How do we cope under such circumstances? I've come to the conclusion that staying emotionally healthy requires us to do three things when a challenge arises:

- *face the truth*
- *acknowledge the problem*
- *assume responsibility to change*

I'd like to illustrate this by relating a story about how I had to do all three of those things when my wife and I faced a personal challenge.

Denise was diagnosed with triple-negative breast cancer. During that time, I found that I was excellent at providing her with *instrumental* support. In other words, if something needed to be done or an appointment needed to be scheduled, I was on top of it. If she was cold or uncomfortable, I'd bring her a blanket or a cup of water.

As far as I was concerned, advances in medicine had our backs. The cancer was stage one, and even though triple-negative is an aggressive type of cancer, my wife's doctors seemed optimistic about her future and treatment plan. I shared in those feelings.

But my wife didn't feel that same confidence. She was afraid of the future and even of dying. We had a new granddaughter to spoil, and Denise was terrified that she wouldn't have the chance to see the little one grow up. I'd tell her that her prospects were great, that surgery had successfully removed the whole tumor, and that her chemo was just preventative.

So I just couldn't understand why she kept crying. I also didn't know what to say or how else to help.

Now I can see what I failed to do that at that point—and it pertained to that "face the truth" bullet point. The truth was that my wife was affected by this health challenge in a way that I didn't *completely* understand. Yes, I love her deeply and was thrown for a loop by the diagnosis, but I hadn't *fully* entered into the reality of how scary this was for Denise. Maybe that's because I wasn't the one who had cancer. Or maybe it was because it was easier for *me* to trust the doctors when they told us that things should turn out OK. In any case, I now understand that I had some spade work to do.

And then my journey took me to the second bullet point: "acknowledge the problem."

The cancer center we went to offered free counseling as part of their treatment. My wife started attending, and then one Friday the counselor asked to speak with me alone before bringing my wife into the session.

What the counselor told me in that session felt like a personal attack—all I could hear was that I wasn't empathetic and wasn't providing Denise with adequate emotional support. When Denise was brought into the meeting, she started crying, and I was so confused.

In that moment, I felt like a failure as a husband. I felt that my whole life had been a sham and that I was a terrible person.

In retrospect, I can see that I had to acknowledge a major problem. The truth was that I didn't provide the right kind of empathy.

My counselor helped me realize that I was gifted at *instrumental* and *informational* support.

But no matter what medications I brought to my wife, no matter how many mouth rinses I prepared, no matter how many blankets I laid across her lap, she was still in a state of distress. My counselor looked at me and said, "Well, Steve, what she's missing is your *emotional* support."

I wanted to be a good husband, so once I faced the truth and accepted the fact that I could do a better job of being sensitive and sharing the journey, I tackled the third bullet point— "assuming responsibility to change." I wanted to get to a place where I could better understand and respond to my wife's emotional needs.

As it turned out, I ended up going through a whole series of counseling sessions that taught me a lot about myself. I embraced the chance to delve into my past and understand why I had certain unhelpful tendencies and behaviors.

I dug into learning everything I could about emotions— how we feel them, which ones I'm better at understanding, how to empathize with others in difficult situations, etc. Through studying emotional intelligence, I found that I scored very well on personal competencies like self-awareness and self-management. But when it came to social-emotional intelligence, I was quite weak.

The beauty of emotional intelligence, however, is that it's a learnable trait. I was able to grow—and over time, I was able to understand my wife's fear and pain. We connected on a deeper level, and it was amazing how much closer it brought us.

The whole experience began in a frightening way but ended up being very positive, and our marriage grew stronger. But the point I'm trying to convey is that emotional awareness and intelligence can be acquired. We can learn and change. In fact, mental balance requires that.

Helping others with their mental balance

So far, we've been focusing on our own individual mental balance. But since we also care about our fellow human beings from a "brother's keeper" perspective, I think we also should think for a moment about how to relate to other people who undoubtedly encounter the same kinds of challenges that we do.

Sometimes when we casually ask people how they're doing, they'll automatically respond, "I'm fine." However, it's often been said that *fine* could be an acronym for "Feeling Insecure, Neurotic and Emotional"!

But mental balance is so personal, so internal, that there's no way to fully know what's happening inside another person's mind. People can get pretty good at masking their true feelings and emotional states. In fact, it seems to me that some of the people who appear to really have it all together are actually among the most confused and needy.

Therefore, we can't assume, based on what people let us see of their lives, that things are as good as they appear. Our coworkers, acquaintances, friends and family members may be in a place of quiet desperation even though they present themselves as being in a very positive place. There's rarely a time when we can know definitively what's happening inside another person's mind.

That's why, in everything we do, we treat others with grace and kindness. We try hard to connect with them and let them know that we're there for support. We try to give them the sense that it's all right to drop the mask and be real with us.

Ultimately, mental balance can be faked, and of course people are responsible for their own internal conditions. But we want to be available to help when we can.

Conclusion

In his book *Victory Over the Darkness*, Neil T. Anderson said, "If what we think does not reflect truth, then what we feel does not reflect reality."

A key theme of this chapter has been that discerning the truth is essential to seeking and achieving mental balance— and everything else follows from that. I hope that's been an enlightening and empowering insight for you. I also hope you've seen very clearly that we are not defined by our struggles, our shortcomings and our perceived failures. Finally, I hope you've become aware of how negative experiences can throw us off balance—and how we can regain that mental balance by reconfiguring our "internal messaging."

For me, mental balance is grounded in the truth of who I am— encompassing my gifts and strengths as well as my shortcomings and negative characteristics. The personality I was given is mine to develop. The life situations I find myself in are mine to face and embrace. My mistakes are mine to be responsible for. I can put it all together and move forward in fearless confidence not because I'm perfect but because I belong to God.

CHAPTER SIX

FINANCIAL BALANCE

"A man wants to earn money in order to
be happy, and his whole effort and the
best of a life are devoted to the earning
of that money. Happiness is forgotten;
the means are taken for the end."

—*Camus*

To say the least, our current society is consumer-driven—or we might even say *money-* driven.

We're bombarded by advertisements every time we watch television, drive down a highway or go online to research something. Depending on what estimate is used, it seems that the average American can be exposed to 10,000 or more ads every day.

Companies spend billions of dollars to research how we think, shop and live, with the goal of influencing our everyday spending choices and contributing to their bottom line. In the materialistic culture we're immersed in, it's easy to see why so many people are lured into debt and fail to make sound decisions about their personal finances.

For many people, one of life's greatest challenges is dealing with money. Good choices can lift them up. Bad choices can drag them down and even have generational consequences.

Naturally, we all want to succeed at personal finance. We want to be prosperous, have the ability to do some good with our resources, and eventually enjoy a comfortable retirement.

The problem is that many people just don't know how to call the plays that will be successful on the financial playing field. They aren't sure how to make choices that will pay off economically. They don't see a way to make money through what they're passionate about. They can't assemble the resources to pursue their dreams, or maybe they're mired in debt and can't find their way out of it.

The underlying challenge is learning and truly understanding how money and finance work.

If we don't master this area, it has implications for every other part of our lives. Even someone who has a high income might have personal finances that are in disarray.

In this chapter, we scrutinize our values, priorities and practices relating to money. We want to make sure that the "American dream" of financial prosperity doesn't turn into a nightmare instead.

How we think about money

We need to have a clear-eyed view of what money is. There's nothing inherently moral or immoral about it. It's merely a medium of exchange. It's a way for our labor (and assets, if we want to sell them) to be converted into cash that can be used to purchase the products and services that we need. The beauty of it is that instead of working on a neighbor's farm in order to procure a chicken from him, we can work in an office or factory and use the money we earn to buy that chicken—and even buy it in the grocery store because of the fungibility of currency.

Money isn't the enemy—but neither is it our salvation. It's neutral.

If someone tells you that "money is the root of all evil," maybe you should kindly correct that person. *Money* isn't the problem. What the Bible verse actually says is that "the *love* of money is the root of all evil" (1 Timothy 6:10, KJV).

Again, money is merely a medium for transmitting value. Problems arise only when our attitudes about it aren't right. For example, maybe we're greedy, or maybe we want to spend money that we don't have by borrowing. Now we could be getting into the danger zone.

As I hope that brief discussion makes clear, financial wellness demands that we understand how money works and what its role in our life is. It's true that a lack of money can create hardship and be a problem, but it's also true that all the money in the world isn't capable of fixing all of our problems. In fact, money can even magnify our problems, depending on the situation.

It seems pretty obvious that the way we handle money can be a reflection of something deeper inside of us. What might be happening inside that we need to own and release? Sometimes it's really hard to be honest with others—and even ourselves—when it comes to money. We may share our scariest, most traumatic burdens with spouses and trusted friends, yet we can be afraid to talk honestly about money.

When I meet with clients to discuss their financial situations, it often becomes obvious that the topic of money makes them feel fearful and ashamed. It can result in severe discomfort for them. That may be an indication that we measure our self-worth by how much money we have. But of course we have to free ourselves of such materialistic thinking.

'Subprime crisis' thunder in the distance

Floods come into our lives in a couple ways. They can arrive all at once as in a catastrophic flash flood or tsunami. Or the water can rise gradually, almost undetected at first— but before long, it can overwhelm us. Both types can be devastating. In my experience, it's especially easy to underestimate the financial floods that slowly rise over time. Some of these floods can be enabled—or stopped dead in their tracks, if we make the right choices—by our values, beliefs and habits.

I was far from alone in experiencing the floodwaters of the so-called subprime mortgage crisis that came to a head in 2007. If you paid attention to those developments, you know of the financial devastation that occurred and afflicted the economy for a decade.

Looking back, I can see that the water started to rise in my own life when I allowed myself to get hooked on the heady feeling of trading in the markets, which were on a rocket ship fueled by speculation and overconfidence.

In the years leading up to the mortgage crisis, I was an active day trader in the stock market.

I was having a great deal of success, earning enough supplemental income that I didn't even need to take a salary from my insurance agency, which also was doing quite well. I read every book I could find about day trading, and I became confident in reading candlestick charts and studying short-term stock trends on a daily basis. I was so confident that I traded with triple margins and on lines of credit.

For those who don't know the term, "trading on margins" basically means you borrow the money you're investing. This is a very risky strategy that enhances the gains while also accelerating the losses—so triple margins triple the profits and also triple the pain when things don't go in the direction you expected. You can get wiped out in a hurry if the markets go south.

Meanwhile, mortgage brokers across the nation were hungry for commissions in a market that was almost saturated. Most qualified homebuyers had already taken the plunge. Brokers then started seeking out prospective buyers who really didn't have the financial wherewithal to purchase a home. People who worked low-paying jobs were qualifying to finance expensive properties without so much as a down payment. This could happen because banks were willing to loan money on a "subprime" basis. This kind of risky loan is given to borrowers weren't well qualified and could easily end up defaulting.

Home sales skyrocketed as subprime mortgages with high interest rates and ballooning payments enabled unwise purchases. Homeowners were happy, brokers were happy, politicians were happy, and I was happy. I was riding high and living the good life for about five years. My pride and ego got wrapped up in a sense of great excitement about all the money I was making. I was on the mountaintop.

Now I can see that the high-rolling game I was playing went to my head. I got careless with my spending. I played more golf than I should have, flying to places like Scottsdale, Arizona, to play some beautiful courses. And while I was day-trading stocks, I also purchased a few additional insurance agencies that further bolstered my income. If I had a problem, I'd just throw money at it. I now understand how someone can be in a cult and not realize they're in a cult. The money and the thrills were intoxicating.

The crisis hits

But the entire financial system was built on a shaky foundation, and the floodwaters started to rise. In 2007, the markets crashed in a spectacular fashion. As the crisis intensified, I lost a lot of money. I remember one day in particular when I watched my account valuations go down in real time. It wasn't funny at the time, but it reminded me of the scene from "National Lampoon's Christmas Vacation" when Chevy Chase plugged in his Christmas lights and the electric meter started spinning out of control.

As the market crashed, pretty much every line of credit I had taken out for trading was called in by the financial institutions. I had margin calls every day. The financial structure I had been using to support my lifestyle was cut off. Even the money I had been saving for my wife to buy a new car was decimated—I lost almost 80% of it. The empire I had been building, the mountain upon which I stood, turned to dust.

Thankfully, most of my clients weren't trading stocks heavily and thus weren't too negatively affected in the days and weeks following the market crash. But it hurt that my brother, who was recovering from a serious car accident, needed the money I had invested for him. Most of it had disappeared in the collapse.

I struggled to make payroll, and as a result, I had to let one employee go and reduce another to half-time status. We cut every possible expense in the office. We all worked a lot harder just to get the same amount of work done. Even though I knew I hadn't been the ultimate cause of the collapse, I was still shrouded in shame and embarrassment. I thought I had been outsmarting the system, but in reality, I was the one being had. Many Americans faced the same challenge, but it was small comfort knowing that I wasn't alone.

Some of my relationships ended up being strained for a time. And in the wreckage, I had to figure out how to rebuild. Hard conversations followed, and I faced the difficult work of reconstructing my life in the months and years to come.

I'd never had my hair turn gray faster than it did following the subprime mortgage crisis. And through the rebuilding process, I came to realize that my happy little place on top of the mountain of stuff I had built wasn't as beautiful as I had initially thought. It was shallow and superficial, and it was never built to last. The foundation was made of sand. Each day of that season had a little more water accumulating at the base of my castle, and each day I was blind to it.

The water seeped into the foundation, weakened my investments, weakened my relationships, and weakened me. And when the tsunami of the financial crash hit, I was devastated.

But alas, the tsunami was not the end. We rebuilt, and this time I made sure that the foundation was solid—and waterproof. No more sandcastles of ego for me.

Big money isn't the answer

It's interesting to consider the apparently common belief that "If I just had a little more money or would win the lottery, I'd be happy." But in fact, about 70% of people who win a lottery or get a big windfall actually end up broke in a few years, according to the National Endowment for Financial Education. Steve Lewit, CEO of Wealth Financial Group, says: "People who were little, ordinary people all of a sudden become extraordinary. They're euphoric. They lose all sense of reality. They think they're invincible and powerful. They think they're Superman."

I've seen this basic phenomenon play out frequently in my 40-plus years of working in financial services. People may possess a significant amount of money, but that doesn't mean they know how to manage it. It might not even contribute to their happiness at any level.

It's natural to spend more money when we have more, but without a budget, it's easy to lose track of how much is spent— and end up underwater. Many don't realize this until it's too late.

A good example of this comes from the world of professional football. Well-known agent Leigh Steinberg wrote in Forbes that 80% of retired NFL players go broke within three years of leaving the game. That might seem unbelievable in light of the fact that NFL salaries seem astronomical to "everyday wage earners" like many of us.

But according to Steinberg, retired players can stumble for a lot of reasons. For example, they lack competent advice in navigating the complexities of taxes and investments, they give away too much of their money to friends and family, or they don't adequately plan for what happens after their playing career comes to an abrupt end.

That's exactly why it's important to be intentional and thoughtful about managing our resources.

Mastering financial literacy

By my calculations, three states (Missouri, Arkansas and New Hampshire) have small communities that are named Success. You can look them up on your GPS and visit them if you like.

But I've never seen a road atlas or GPS map capable of helping us find an easy route to a place called *Financial Success*. For one thing, that destination will be different for all of us. And whatever route we take, we're likely to encounter roadblocks and hazards along the way.

Yes, lightning can strike—someone can win the lottery or be the recipient of huge inheritance. That can take care of the money part of success. But as we know, there's more to achieving financial success than merely accumulating money.

True success comes from acquiring resources *and* having the right mindset about them. That's a totally different thing than just madly chasing after wealth. The right path demands endurance, grit, desire, passion, struggle, loss and—maybe above all—the correct spirit. But eventually, it's the path that makes everything worthwhile.

Many people never achieve balance in their finances because they don't master the fundamentals or they get discouraged for one reason or another. We aren't born with an understanding of money, and most people never take the time to learn. To achieve financial balance, we need to get up to speed on some important aspects of managing money. With financial wisdom and discipline, we can overcome any fears, anxieties and obstacles that stand between us and a sound financial position.

It always has amazed me that while finance is a central part of our lives, most people never really master basic financial concepts. They never achieve what we might call "financial literacy."

But no one will do this for us, so we need to take care of business ourselves. Maybe you've heard the important formula that consists of 10 two-letter words: "If it is to be, it is up to me."

Don't let adversity hamper growth

As a Toastmaster, I once gave a talk based on Tony Robbins' "Five Keys to Wealth and Happiness." The idea is that, with mastery of each of these keys, everyone will have the tools to pursue excellence and, in turn, wealth and happiness.

I encourage you to look up all five "keys"—they're worth investigating. Here, though, I want to highlight two of them that I think are especially important. At first it may seem as if these two keys don't have anything much to do with personal finances, but they actually do— they speak to the issue of money and our relationship to it.

The first key is developing the ability to handle rejection. Of course, rejection happens to all of us. I've experienced this in many aspects of life, just as you have.

But here's the thing about it. The fear of rejection does far more harm than the rejection itself. Why? Because if we're afraid to pursue opportunities, we shut ourselves off from the possibility of growth—in finances and in other ways. Being frozen in fear means that we don't take risks, and without risk, we aren't likely to make any progress. Sometimes hearing the word "no" is essential to learning the lessons we need to learn so that we can move ahead.

There's a secondary aspect of rejection that also is worthy of consideration. I'll admit that I've spent a fair amount of time being wrapped up in anxiety and fear of rejection. For example, maybe I worried about being passed over for a promotion or being told no by a potential client.

But I've learned that rejection isn't the end of the road. I know of a young woman who, just out of college, applied for an editing job at a major publishing house. When she was "rejected" for that position, it was discouraging. But a few weeks later, the company called back and offered her a higher- level (and higher-paying) job. It was a good thing she didn't give up at the first sign of rejection.

Actually, I've come to see that in a way, rejection can be freeing. It frees me to rethink what success looks like and has the power to put me on a new path—or *force* me to seek out a new path.

Yes, rejection can be painful in the short term, but if we approach it with the right attitude, it can contribute to the kind of financial success that this chapter is all about.

Giving generously

The second key from Tony Robbins is simple enough, but it's truly foundational to achieving financial balance and forging the proper relationship with our money and other resources.

That key is to give more than we expect to receive—to be generous. Doing this reinforces the idea that money is not something to be hoarded, nor is it meant simply for our own selfish uses. Instead, we should see our resources as being entrusted to us for good stewardship.

If you've spent time reading the Bible, you probably recognize this as a biblical principle. Perhaps the best expression of it is in Luke 6:38, where Jesus says: "Give, and it will be given to you. A good measure, pressed down, shaken together and running over, will be poured into your lap. For with the measure you use, it will be measured to you" (NIV).

Esau, the easy fix and financial wisdom

I once delivered a speech called "The Esau Syndrome." If you paid attention in Sunday school, you probably remember the Old Testament story of Esau and Jacob. Esau was the first- born son and thus the one entitled to a hefty birthright of land and money.

But younger brother Jacob wanted Esau's birthright—and was incredibly crafty. Jacob made a pot of stew one day while Esau was off hunting, and when the famished Esau returned, he begged Jacob for a bowl. Jacob, sensing the desperation of his brother, said, "Only if you give me your birthright." So Esau, in a moment of hunger and weakness, traded away immense future blessings for a bowl of stew.

I can't count the number of times in my life that I've been Esau and traded away some future benefit for the rush of getting something lesser that I wanted right now. We do this in the drive-thru at the burger joint, at the grocery store and when we shop online. Instead of taking the long view and making wise decisions, we rashly spend money on everything from junk food and frivolous trinkets to expensive "toys" that don't truly bring happiness. Some of our spending decisions tend to be based on instant gratification rather than thoughtful, intentional budgeting and financial planning. Perhaps we buy things because of the way they stroke our egos or make us look good on social media.

Or maybe we think a gadget or toy has the ability to satisfy some deep-seated felt need or change us for the better. But that idea is utterly false. Money won't make us better or happier. It merely magnifies who we already are. An angry, selfish person who inherits a lot of money will remain angry and selfish—just with more money. And if someone who is generous and charitable inherits money, that person is simply going to have more money to give away.

In the grand scheme of things, money is important only to the extent that it allows us to enjoy things that we believe are important. We need to keep this in perspective. Having a grasp on our money and our financial situation, and being able to not worry about money, is critical to living a fulfilling life. It's not about how much we have in the bank—it's about the way we understand and view what's in the bank.

'The Goose & the Golden Egg'

There's an Aesop's fable that often comes to mind when I think about money and especially productivity. Everyone knows the story as "The Goose and the Golden Egg." In case it's been a while since you were immersed in children's literature, here's a refresher course—actually, the whole tale:

> *There was once a Countryman who possessed the most wonderful Goose you can imagine, for every day when he visited the nest, the Goose had laid a beautiful, glittering, golden egg.*
>
> *The Countryman took the eggs to market and soon began to get rich. But it was not long before he grew impatient with the Goose because she gave him only a single golden egg a day. He was not getting rich fast enough.*
>
> *Then one day, after he had finished counting his money, the idea came to him that he could get all the golden eggs at once by killing the Goose and cutting it open. But when the deed was done, not a single golden egg did he find, and his precious Goose was dead.*

Naturally, every fable has a moral, and this one is easy to see: Those who have plenty want more and so lose all they have.

Let's begin our analysis of this tale by observing that it's natural for us to identify with the farmer, who obviously has financial needs. It's the same for us. Obligations and expectations are imposed upon us—those we have for ourselves as well as those that others have for us. We must tend to our jobs, our families, our bank accounts, our extensive to-do lists. There's a lot of pressure there, and it usually involves finance and productivity. For a while, the "golden goose" is the farmer's meal ticket, and we can understand why he'd like to get right at the source of all the gold.

But we also can identify with the goose. Think of it this way. Like the golden goose, we have the power to produce greatness. When we nurture ourselves properly, we are capable of accomplishing great things—"golden eggs" in different forms.

The point of the fable, however, is that the farmer has a character flaw that brings the whole profitable arrangement to a swift and bitter end—and of course that flaw is greed. The short-sighted farmer tried to short-circuit the traditional approach to accumulating wealth, and it ended up costing him dearly in the long run.

When productivity is on the line, results clearly matter. That's what we strive for. But what matters more is the process— fertilizing the land, tilling the soil, and watering the field in order to produce abundant crops. We can't neglect that process in favor of some "get rich quick" scheme.

Of sports cars and wise choices

Ego-based spending reflects our mental and spiritual state and may stem from greed, extravagance, rebellion, feelings of inferiority and a number of other unhealthy impulses. Such materialistic spending gives the illusion of happiness and can be hard to resist.

This isn't to deny that a boat, RV or vacation home can't bring a lot of joy to someone's life. But we can't be misled into thinking that the endless pursuit of "toys" and material goods will make us happy.

To be honest, I've battled the spending impulse many times, and I enjoy a nice car as much as the next guy. For 14 years, I drove a shiny black Infiniti G35. Even up until the time I got rid of it, it remained a daily pleasure to drive. It was a sleek, sporty gem of craftsmanship. When people saw me drive up in it, the car always elicited admiration and compliments. I loved how it looked and how it made me feel.

But when the constant electrical issues forced me to give up the vehicle, I made the practical move toward a sedan. It was a nice car, too, but it just didn't give me the same feeling as the Infiniti.

It's interesting to contemplate how we can have an unhealthy, ego-based attachment to a pile of metal, rubber and plastic. And we can come up with all kinds of rationalizations to make ourselves feel better about these purchases. Maybe we say that the car doesn't depreciate as quickly or that it has superior performance in crash tests. But at the end of the day, we know the truth: We want to feel special, and we want people to look at us and think, "Wow—that person really made it." That's the epitome of ego spending.

We need to realize, however, that our financial balance (and personal character, for that matter) is never improved by spending on things that do nothing more than inflate our ego. We have to discern when we're in danger of spending money on something because of pride rather than utility.

Ego-based spending is inherently rooted in comparisons— what we used to call "keeping up with Joneses." And when we're caught up in a wave of who has the better "stuff," we end up disconnected from our principles and the things we truly value. Money is a magnifier. If we value being perceived as better than others, then the way we spend money will reflect that belief.

As I suggested above, this doesn't mean—at least in my mind— that we can't enjoy a nice home, car or speed boat. Everyone has to rely on his or her own conscience, but we probably don't have to live in a tent and walk five miles to work every day.

What I'm trying to say is that we have to bring discipline and discernment to our financial choices. By taking an honest look at our motivations for spending, we enable ourselves to make better decisions. These will be decisions that don't feed our ego but instead are grounded in making wise investments, living within our means, and avoiding unnecessary debt to the best of our ability. The main thing is to recognize that our worth is not found in how much stuff we can accumulate. That's a critical step in reorienting the way we think about and use money.

And now I have to confess that there's a postscript to the car story. I drove my Lexus four- door sedan—what family members teasingly called my "grandpa car"—for three years. But the temptation to drive a sportier car was just too great, and I gave in. Maybe this is a blind spot or area of weakness for me. Maybe it's ego (but I hope not). Maybe I just love the feel of a fun and speedy sports car when I'm driving. But somehow, I ended up with an Infiniti Q60 coupe in my driveway.

I was tempted to say that we're all human, it's hard to be perfect, and thanks for understanding. But that would imply that it's a financial *transgression* to buy something that we enjoy. That would be the wrong message. The right message is to choose wisely—and not spend money on reckless indulgences.

Mastering the basics of accounting

In chapter 3, we briefly mentioned Socrates and his "know thyself" principle. But what he left out was the importance of also knowing thy income and net-worth statements.

This takes us into the sticky area of accounting. Some people seem to have a knack for balance sheets and the like. Others, not so much. I was in the latter category during college—until a caring professor and the 3x5 card rescued me.

As a sophomore in college, I naturally had to take a number of required courses for my degree in marketing. Three of them were in accounting.

The first time through Accounting 201, I felt like I was trying to learn a foreign language. I struggled and dropped the class. But if I didn't pass 201, I wouldn't be able to take 202 and 203—and finish my major.

I signed up for 201 a second time. I studied long and hard, but I received an F. Now feeling stupid, I took the class for a third time. The pressure was on. If I didn't pass, I wouldn't earn my degree.

Two weeks into the class, I went to the professor and explained that I just wasn't "getting it." I'll always remember what she told me. She explained that I simply needed to memorize the different accounting statements along with what accounts go into each statement. She recommended that I make 3x5 flash cards and spend a lot of time drilling myself.

That was easy for me to do because I already considered the humble 3x5 card the Swiss Army knife of an organized life. I memorized what the professor told me to master, and I ended up with an A in the course—and an A in the other two courses as well. (Maybe the word "grit" comes to mind here.)

My advice to balance-seeking readers is to follow the same advice that accounting professor gave me many years ago: Learn and understand the net-worth statement and the cash-flow statement. I'll explain them in the next section. But without the essential data contained in these statements, it'll be difficult to get a handle on your budget, retirement and overarching sense of financial balance.

The net-worth and cash-flow statements

Let's take a little voyage in a pirate ship. Imagine that we've made our way to a deserted island that has a buried treasure. We have an "X marks the spot" map, so we're eager to drop anchor, hobble around the island on our peg legs, and see what we can find.

We extensively discussed goals in chapter 3, so I think the reader is well-versed in their importance. On our pirate-ship adventure, the obvious goal is clearly the little patch of ground that corresponds to the "X." And the map will help us get to the right location.

Is there a similar map for charting our financial course? Yes. Actually, there are many, but I want to highlight the aforementioned net-worth and cash-flow statements. These are the starting points for financial understanding.

The net-worth statement, which is really a personal balance sheet, is divided into two columns. On the left are your assets (investments, car, home, personal items), and on the right are your liabilities (mortgage, student loan, consumer debt, etc.).

This statement is imperative if you want to know what your overall financial status is. Constant awareness of your balance sheet prepares you to make wise decisions. It doesn't matter if you're a wealthy movie star, an NFL phenom or an average Joe (or Josephine)—awareness is the key to keeping your financial situation balanced, and the net-worth statement gives you a handle on that.

The second accounting fundamental is your cash-flow statement. This also can be called an income statement or even a basic budget. Here, you create an in-depth analysis of your income and your expenditures.

On the side of the ledger designated for income, most people probably would start by listing the total wages they earn every month. But if you have other types of income, you need to list them here as well. Perhaps you earn a little money by doing some freelance work, renting out an apartment, or selling crafts or collectibles on an auction site.

And then the flip side of the coin is to list all your expenditures. Be warned that it can take some work to compile these numbers— and even when you think you have a complete list, other expenses inevitably crop up.

But try to list all the money that flows out of the household, including groceries, gasoline, cable TV, cellphones, insurance, automobile repairs, retirement contributions, charitable giving, utilities and entertainment.

Remember, however, that a lot of the money we spend doesn't show up on a regular monthly basis. For example, if you're making a budget in February, you're probably not thinking to set aside money for Christmas presents, a vacation or a new set of tires. These are expenses we often forget about, and as a result, when they sneak up on us, we may be left scrambling to find the necessary cash. Therefore, it's not a bad idea to go through the family budget archives (which might simply be a box of receipts) and anticipate as many of those irregular expenses as possible.

The cash-flow statement is both a monthly budgeting tool and a long-term annual planning instrument. It's simple enough to create and maintain this document, but it's astonishing how many people neglect doing so—or perhaps don't even have a grasp of why this kind of number- crunching is important.

You can take your personal financial analysis to a much higher level if you wish. There are a lot of sophisticated tools and software packages available. But everyone should master the net- worth and cash-flow statements. Without them, financial balance could be elusive—like the buried treasure that a map-less pirate can't find.

These two statements are the cornerstone of financial guru Dave Ramsey's five books. After filing bankruptcy in 1988, Dave built a $200-million-dollar "Financial Peace" business—based largely on the commonsense perspective of these two statements. They may be simple to learn, but they're difficult to live out. It takes discipline.

Three principles of financial planning

In addition to highlighting the value of net-worth and cash-flow statements, we want to examine three principles of financial planning that also are imperative to managing money successfully.

The first is that we must be able to think long term. The longer our planning horizon, the better the financial decisions we'll be able to make.

That's within reason, of course. Granted, if you're just graduating from college at age 22, it would be premature to start working out exactly what your travel budget will be during your retirement years. But it certainly wouldn't be premature to plan ahead for home ownership and maybe having children—and even to think about retirement at some level.

I encourage my clients to start saving money for retirement at an early age. There's no substitute for the power of money that earns interest over a long period of time.

Here's an example. If you save $300 a month between the ages of 25 and 65, and if you earn a 10% average return (about what the Standard and Poor's 500 index has done over the past 100 years), you'd be able to stash away $1,913,034.07 by age 65.

Many people pay everybody else first and then, if they're lucky, save whatever they might have left. That's why the average American dies with $62,000 of debt. But for about $10 a day, we can create a bulwark of retirement security.

Growing financial assets can be compared to planting and cultivating an apple tree. You don't expect to plant a seed today and harvest the fruit and enjoy the shade tomorrow. Instead, the seed germinates, becomes a small plant, grows over time, and eventually culminates in a fruit-bearing tree. That's an excellent metaphor for what long-term planning and investing are like. But it all begins with planting the seed. Don't delay.

The second principle seems obvious enough: We must spend less than we earn. To meet this goal, we need to know what we're earning and spending—so we need to keep working that cash- flow statement.

I advise people to write down everything they spend money on— at least until they get a handle on their spending and their budget. Yes, you know the amount of your monthly car payment. But how much do you spend on miscellaneous purchases at the coffee shop, the pharmacy, the office superstore?

Over time, seemingly small, inconsequential purchases add up to big money, so it's important to track them. When we don't know where our money is going, it's a lot easier to fall into the trap of living beyond our means. But when our spending is spelled out in black and white, it's easier to spot the problem areas.

Our third principle is to maintain a savings account for emergencies.

This account should be kept separate from our retirement savings and is intended to help us deal with the surprises that life throws our way.

How much should we have in an emergency fund? A general rule of the thumb is to set aside enough money so that we could get by for at least three months—and more would be ideal. These funds should be maintained in a liquid account so we don't have to pay a penalty to get access to them.

An emergency fund would be critical to our financial survival if, heaven forbid, we suddenly lose our job or have some other unanticipated setback. We also can draw on it if we have to suddenly replace a car or major appliance. An emergency fund is an essential component of a strong financial position, so it shouldn't be neglected.

Aligning financial decisions with our values

We've now established how important it is to incorporate the "three principles" and the net- worth and cash-flow statements into our plan for financial balance. But as we wrap up this chapter, we also need to reinforce the idea that there must be congruence between our values and the way we earn, spend and invest our money.

Values, goals and priorities are foundational to our personal finances. We must begin with a clear understanding of these elements before we can make wise choices about our resources.

This, I believe, is where financial planners often go wrong—they go straight to dollar signs and skip the most important part, which is discerning what their clients value the most. Over many years of meeting with thousands of clients, I've learned to begin by asking what's important to *them* about their money. And then I ask them why that is. This shines the spotlight on what people truly value.

When I start working with a new client, I'll ask questions that illuminate their values and beliefs about earning, managing and spending money. I might even ask what their parents' concept of money was. This helps establish a baseline understanding for both parties—for the client as well as for me, the adviser. In any other arena of life, we'd naturally try to understand the essential background before we start making decisions. But some people don't apply that process to their finances, which obviously is a huge mistake. It's possible—even necessary—to approach money and finance from a thoughtful, self-aware perspective.

If financial decisions aren't grounded in clear thinking about the things that are most important to us, we won't end up where we want to be. Frustration abounds when expectations are not being met. Purpose, meaning and understanding are the keys.

We don't have to be financial geniuses to live a financially balanced life. For some, financial stability has never seemed possible because they've never acquired and mastered the tools to make it happen for themselves. But you are capable, and you can do this. It comes down to winning the day-to-day battle—the Esau syndrome inside us all—and understanding and living out our most deeply held values.

To value or not to value

Sometimes the values in a society can get out of balance. For example, the self-storage industry in the United States has always amazed me. In the last 50 years, that sector has boomed to the point where it's a $40 billion industry—with one in 11 Americans paying almost $100 a month just to store their extra stuff. It's estimated that these storage units are crammed with 2.3 billion square feet of old furniture, old appliances and old holiday decorations. That's enough to fill Lake Mead 26 times—and it doesn't even take into account the stuff that people have in their garages, attics, basements and sheds.

Contrast that with the fact that we have something like 500,000 homeless people living in America—25% of whom are children and 10% of whom are veterans. We could very well have 80 storage units for every homeless person in the United States. What's wrong with that ratio? What does it say about us? Do we value stuff over people?

The life-changing potential of a simple question

Our minds have a way of remembering things that are associated with strong emotions and images. I remember one day back in 1976, when I was a senior at Marion High School. I had taken my place in the stereotypical science lab, complete with the stools and the black tables. I got to class early one day. My teacher was wearing his white lab coat. I was sporting my long, stringy hair, bellbottom jeans and a pack of Kool cigarettes in my pocket.

Naturally, cigarettes were not allowed in school. But instead of confronting me directly and sending me to the principal's office, the teacher approached me like a friend and said, "Hey, did you see the new poster on the bulletin board in the back of the room?" He asked me to go check it out.

Burned out, spaced out and confused (my normal state of being), I wandered back and looked at the big, glossy poster. It featured photographs of a smoker's lung (black, shrunken and ugly) and the healthy lung of a non-smoker. As I stared at the contrasting images, I realized why the teacher had sent me back there—he had noticed my cigarettes.

The power of that picture created an urge in me to walk up to the trash can and throw away those cancer sticks. I never smoked another cigarette.

Sometimes I think about how that teacher's simple question— "Did you see the poster?"—had a lifelong impact on me. It changed my perspective and perhaps saved my life, and I'm very grateful for that.

But the point is that the experience helped me understand how a good question can change your life. Many great teachers realize this, which is why they use the Socratic method.

I've had many excellent teachers in my life, but the ones I remember most are the ones who peppered the class with questions. (One day I said to a teacher, "Why do you ask so many questions?" He responded, "What's wrong with a good question?")

In my 40 years of helping clients achieve financial balance, I've found that questions play a vital role in helping us understand our relationship with money. Therefore, I'm going to close this chapter with a series of questions that have served me well. This approach works as effectively with ultra-rich clients as it does with clients who are just scraping by.

The system consists of three phases, three questions in each phase, and three action steps to take.

Phase one: Understanding yourself

- *What is important to you about your money?*
- *Why is it important?*
- *What are your beliefs, values and priorities pertaining to money?*

Step one: Brainstorm these questions. Take as much time as you need. Write your answers on a piece of paper.

Step two: Seek a reality coach and an unbiased financial adviser, especially if you have special circumstances (for example, maybe you're a professional athlete or you make a lot of money in some other way).

Step three: Spend some time focusing on the "know thyself " principle. Money is currency, and you need to understand its flow in your life.

Phase two: Understanding your reality

- *What happens when life's uncertainties come your way?*
- *On the map of life, do you know where you are?*
- *Can you see the whole map and all the potential hazards?*

Step one: Consider the three major possibilities for the way your life may unfold. You may live a very long time, you may die prematurely, or you may suffer illness or injury and need support. Sometimes sharing the risk with an insurance company is the best option.

Step two: Maintain clarity on your financial situation. Net-worth and cash-flow statements need to be created and then reviewed every year. You'll see that some assets will appreciate in value while others will depreciate. It's important to understand why these changes in value happen.

Step three: Take in the big picture, like you would if you consulted a road atlas or electronic map when planning a cross-country road trip. Be alert to potential hazards in your financial journey. Break each aspect of your finances into smaller parts, understand each part, improve each part, and then put the improved parts back together for a greater whole. Follow the formula, "whole, parts, whole."

Phase three: Understanding your vision

- *What is your time horizon—short-term, mid-range or long-range?*
- *Do you need a second opinion or professional guidance? Look for someone you can connect with and who has experience, proper motives and good moral character.*
- *What are your financial goals, financial priorities and desired milestones? Step one:* Group your goals and priorities into three time frames:
- *short-term (present to one year)*
- *mid-range (from one to five years)*

- *long-range (up to 50 years, depending on your age)*

Step two: Set up safety nets, insurance coverage and good investments that have guaranteed returns.

Step three: Execute all the necessary legal paperwork: wills, trusts and a letter of final instructions. Review these documents every year, and update them as changing life circumstances dictate.

People who answer these questions and follow the associated steps will dramatically improve their chances of achieving financial balance.

PART III

ENERGY

Here's a riddle from an old game called MindTrap: What is at the beginning of eternity, the end of time, the beginning of every end, and the end of every place? Stay tuned for the answer.

When we pull into a gas station these days, we might groan a little bit if the price has gone up or if all the pumps are taken. But imagine if an energy shortage led to riots by panicked drivers who couldn't find a drop of gas. Or if the line to buy fuel was miles long. Or if fights broke out as people fought over who was going to pump the gas next.

If you haven't been around as long as I have, you might not recognize all of that—and more—as being historical fact. The energy crisis of the 1970s took place when I was in high school and college, so I remember it well. I hope we don't have to revisit that kind of crisis and social unrest anytime soon.

Energy is front and center today, too. There's a lot of talk about energy shortages, high prices, renewables, the transition to electric vehicles and so on.

This third and final section of the book also is about energy—but not the kind of energy that lights our houses and powers our cars. It's about harnessing the energy we need to power our lives inward, outward and upward. After all, if we know on an intellectual level the right way to live but don't have the energy to implement it, it doesn't do us a lot of good. Let's take the last step of the journey.

Oh, by the way: The answer to the riddle in the first paragraph is the letter "e."

CHAPTER SEVEN

INWARD ENERGY

He gives strength to the weary and
increases the power of the weak.
Even youths grow tired and weary,
and young men stumble and fall;
but those who hope in the Lord
will renew their strength.
They will soar on wings like eagles;
they will run and not grow weary,
they will walk and not be faint.
—*Isaiah 40:29-31 (NIV)*

Still a college student in 1979, I returned for a third summer of selling Bibles and children's books as a door-to-door salesman for the Southwestern Company. As far as summers go, it was the greatest of my life.

Three of us lived in a big old house with a very nice lady who rented us a few rooms. My roommates Dan and Ron were graduate students at a private college. They were mature salesman, and I observed how they stayed more focused because their tuition was more expensive than mine—they couldn't afford to get off pace.

My first summer with Southwestern had been very successful, but I lost ground during my second summer because of some distractions. This third time around, I was really focused, and I was getting the hang of selling, working hard and staying motivated.

The movie "Rocky II" had just come out, and I was living with some very positive guys.

They listened to Christian music every morning. I hadn't known there was such a thing. But it had a good beat, so I ran with it and even enjoyed it.

I started the summer with a strong performance. My sales were soaring, and I made some good money.

Then for some reason, I got stuck in the doldrums in the middle of the summer. My attitude turned from positive to dark. I just couldn't get pumped up anymore to sell Bibles and children's books for 13 and a half hours a day.

Yes, surrounded by rah-rah salesmen in a can-do organization, I could fake it—but I knew something was just not right inwardly.

I suppose we all go through periods in our lives when we aren't operating at peak efficiency, but this feeling in the summer of '79 seemed to be more of an existential crisis. I didn't immediately understand that it had spiritual roots.

Up to this point in my life, I hadn't made any kind of spiritual commitment. Nevertheless, I could speak a little bit of the lingo when it suited my purposes. It's easier to sell big, coffee-table family Bibles when you can talk the talk, even if you don't walk the walk.

Over time, I became skilled at discerning what people from different denominations wanted to hear in a sales pitch. For example, I could tell if the most effective pitch would involve talking about salvation, the Holy Spirit or "end times." I'd agree with whatever the customer thought— this superficial bonding experience could sell more Bibles.

But I had no real religious convictions of my own. I had gone to church maybe a handful of times in my life, and I always thought the Bible was kind of hard to believe as well as very boring.

I remember in high school when I gave a girl a ride home because she lived on my side of town. She used to party with us, but then she became what we called a "Jesus freak." As I drove her home, she was talking about being saved. And I remember thinking, "Giving up weed and drinking? You're crazy!" I loved my "freedom." However, I also remembered how peaceful, contented, and happy this girl was.

I remember another time in college when an older sales manager had showed me a "plan of salvation" booklet. I remember feeling very uncomfortable, and I told him I was not ready to make any kind of commitment. I always thought such things were for weak and dependent people.

I did believe that there was a God—or at least some kind of higher power in the universe.

And when you spend 80 hours a week for three summers being a door-to-door Bible salesman, you can't avoid having conversations about many spiritual matters. Is Christianity true? Was Jesus real? Where do you go when you die? Is there a judgment day?

Customers often asked me what I believed, and I'd always sidestep the question because I didn't want to lose a sale. But these conversations and questions haunted my mind that summer.

What happened that Thursday

The confusion began to surface in a serious way, and by Thursday, July 26, 1979, it had reached a fever pitch.

It was just outside of Lancaster, South Carolina, and I was working a few subdivisions. My roommate Ron had dropped me off, and I started knocking on doors a little before 8 a.m., as usual. It turned out to be very hot and humid that day—not surprising for July in the south. And when you're a door-to- door salesman on a brutally hot day, you need to get in the customer's house to get cooled off.

Well, on that particular day, nothing was working, and I ran out of energy very early. That was a bit strange since I was only 21 years old and in great physical condition. I read an inspirational "Don't Quit" poem and tried to get going. I had just received a care package from home, which normally would motivate me for a while—but it wasn't helping on that day.

I knew something wasn't right. It seemed to be a mental thing, but it also was affecting my body. This sick, disabling feeling just would not go away that day.

Mohammad Ali is credited with saying, "Often it isn't the mountains ahead that wear you out—it's the little pebble in your shoe." Well, my feet were hurting because of a blister, it seemed like it was 110 degrees, I had no sales, and I felt chained to the ground—or like I was walking in quicksand.

My mental condition was even worse than my physical one. I was lost, confused and discontented. I felt an urgent need to get my head right. It was 11:30, and I had one more hour to complete the first of three four-and-a-half-hour selling periods. I had reached a stretch of road with no houses, and the next subdivision was way up on top of a hill. It probably was a half mile away, but it looked like a journey of a million miles to me. And I didn't have the energy to take another step.

The mental baggage was so heavy that I had to stop. I could barely move. Finally, I saw a small cluster of trees and a little dirt path to a shady spot. Perfect—it was just what I needed to escape the turmoil I was experiencing. The spot even had a small stream and a large log that I could rest on.

I sat down to talk things over with the God I didn't know. I said: "I surrender. I can't go on without your help. I'm not going to leave this spot until you give me some answers."

I pulled out one of the Bibles from my sales kit and started reading, and I went through some prayers—but nothing happened.

I kept reading—still nothing. Where is the peace and abundant life? By now I was crying, unable to move, begging for help—but still nothing.

I must have been quite a sight. I was sick of who I was. I was living in a hell of my own making, and I was powerless to get out. I had read all the promises, and I was starting to believe, but I still wasn't right. It seemed like God was turning a deaf ear to me. I felt like I had failed at everything, and now I was stuck in this unbearable, uncomfortable and broken state of being. I had read the prayer, and it said I'd be saved. But still nothing!

Well, I figured I wasn't in any shape to walk up the hill and try to sell more Bibles, so I decided to take a nap in the quiet, cool oasis I had found.

Then I awoke with a start. It was almost 5:00, and I had slept for three hours. I had spent a total of five hours in this spot. But when I awakened, I felt that I wasn't alone. Something was different.

I started to think about what a great little spot we had found. Wait—did I frame that in terms of *we*? I began to realize that I wasn't alone—that my Creator was with me in this spot...and in me...and everywhere.

The Bible was still on my sales case, and I picked it up and started to read again. This time I began to understand what I was reading. My own strength and resources were gone, but I seemed to be plugged in to a new kind of energy. Now I trusted. Now I believed. Now I understood.

Wow. Yes, I absolutely surrendered my self-sufficiency. I gave myself up and allowed God to start working through me. I realized that I wasn't the Creator—just the created. So if I was in control, I'd really be out of control. I got it. As I read the Bible, I did so with a soft and open heart. I recognized that Jesus paid the price so I could be redeemed. I began to understand that I was saved from myself... accepted and secure...free.

I can still recall what it was like to be in that moment. I started to really feel the energy—not only inside me but all around me. I was the happiest person in the world. But could this gift be for real? Had I just been changed? Were the promises really true?

I went back to the Bible and read some passages just to make sure I really understood. It seemed much better than I imagined. The energy was so powerful, so indescribable, and it coursed through every part of my body. I kept reading, and I felt more power, more energy, more peace. I couldn't stop smiling and praising God.

Then I realized that I had to get to work because I was sitting on a goose egg for the day. But for some reason that didn't matter now. I was just so happy I didn't care. The heat hadn't abated, but I felt fine. I started marching up the big hill to the next subdivision, but I felt like I was Danny Kaye skipping along in "White Christmas." I was so light on my feet that I'm still not sure if my feet were touching the ground.

When I got to the top of the hill, I saw a little house that had a staircase maybe 30 feet up.

Conquering it was no problem with the energy I now had. When I got to the door, a very nice lady said, "Come on in—do I know you?" I told her what had just happened, and then she told me her story. We laughed and talked, and she bought a Bible and fed me a nice meal.

This subdivision turned into a gold mine from a sales perspective. I had seven more sales that evening, and when I started back down that hill around 9:30, I was thinking what a fun evening I'd had. There had been an amazing transformation in my attitude.

When I walked by that little clump of trees, I wondered how I could have spent five hours there. No one could have suspected that I ever got off schedule when I had eight transactions on my sales report.

I learned a lot—indeed, I changed my entire life's direction—on that summer day in South Carolina. I was transformed, I was given a new identity as a child of God, and I found a source of inward energy that has fueled my life ever since.

Now, that was a pretty long story. But that experience in 1979 set the stage for what I've learned throughout my life with respect to "inward energy." We must have this kind of energy if we're going to persevere through an entire lifetime of the kinds of demands, challenges and stresses that we're bound to encounter.

What is inward energy, exactly?

I'm sure I need to be more specific about what "inward energy" is. This isn't a term you'll find in the dictionary (at least not yet!), so I'll try to play the role of Webster here.

I define inward energy as that source of inner motivation, peace and confidence that keeps us physically energized, mentally focused and spiritually aligned. The number of hours in a day is fixed, but the amount of inward energy we can draw on isn't. This essential resource is renewable and plenteous in supply if we know how to tap into and cultivate it.

It might be helpful to think of professional athletes in this context. Of course, athletes who want to stay at the top of their game have to make sure they attend to their physical energy. They need to eat nutritious food, get plenty of rest, and do the other things that keep them physically ready to compete. If they're out partying every night, it won't be long before their energy level will be impacted and their performance will deteriorate.

But athletes also have to nurture their inward energy. The legends find a way to get psyched up for every competition. It doesn't matter if they're in a marquee matchup for the national championship or if they're on the road against the worst team in the league. Either way, they're remarkably good at summoning the focus, strength and even courage they need to perform at the highest level.

That's what inward energy is all about. Our daily work may not involve "clocking in" at a 60,000-seat stadium, but we are no less in need of inward energy than a professional athlete. Maybe we need it even more!

A three-dimensional phenomenon

By now we're used to thinking about concepts in terms of the "triangle effect" and groups of three. You won't be surprised that the template also applies to the important ideas in this chapter, and you probably noticed in the previous section that I referred to how inward energy can keep us "physically energized, mentally focused and spiritually aligned." Well, I do believe that inward energy is three-dimensional in that it has physical, mental and spiritual aspects. Let's take them one at a time.

First, the physical. You'll recall that in chapter four, we focused on how important it is to take care of our physical bodies. Well, there happens to be a connection between that principle and the kind of inward energy we're discussing in this chapter. When we keep our bodies operating at peak efficiency (and we know this will vary from person to person—we're not all triathletes), we have the mental sharpness and motivation to achieve things that we otherwise couldn't.

You know what Ben Franklin said about this, right? "Watching TV and eating potato chips all evening doesn't make people healthy, wealthy or wise—or give them the energy to achieve big things in life." Well, maybe that's not *exactly* the way he put it. But it's probably not much of a stretch to interpret his famous aphorism as implying that physical balance fuels inward energy.

Second, we have the mental aspect. Again, we worked through an entire chapter focused on mental balance, and we can easily trace a vital connection between that and inward energy. Do we cultivate a mental state that's scattered and negative or focused and positive? Where are we on the continuum from unaware to mindful to fully aware? Obviously, we want to be focused, positive and fully aware or engaged. If that's the kind of head space we're in, the inward energy is more likely to flow.

Third, we have the spiritual dimension. Imagine that spirituality is at the top of the pyramid, capping off the physical and mental aspects of inward energy. If we fail to see the world through the lens of faith, we're prone to experiencing the doldrums. As the crews of sailing ships know very well, there's no movement when the doldrums strike because there's no wind power to catch the sails. The result is stagnation.

In contrast, we want to be dialed in spiritually so we're animated by truth, purpose and action. There's nothing more important than understanding our ultimate mission in life—our connection with the sacred—and then following the path that takes us there. This moves us from being uncommitted to being committed.

We can think of our spiritual journey in terms of (a) where we've been—the past, which it's too late do anything about, (b) what course of action is needed in the present, which we *can* do something about, and (c) where we're going—the future, our ultimate destination. But we balance that perspective with the knowledge that God is beyond time and can't be measured by our standards. We remain firm in the belief that there's a dimension to life that is greater than human understanding.

What are the manifestations of inward energy?

Another way to put that question is, How do we recognize inward energy when we see it? I start with the premise that our "external world" reflects our "internal world" to a significant degree. If we want to change the external reality that we live in, we need to start by changing our inner world.

By nature, we have a body, mind and spirit. Naturally, the body takes physical form. It is composed of matter, which is limited by the dimensions of time and space.

Now let's talk about the spirit of a person. Does our spirit have a physical form? Since the answer is no, our spirit is not limited by the dimensions of time and space. Therefore, our spirit can exist in the past, present, and future—it has no boundaries of space, time or knowledge.

This paradox can lead to confusion if we're not aware of how perception works. Our thoughts cause our brains to secrete biochemicals that influence our bodily systems. The function of the brain and nervous system is to interpret environmental stimuli and send signals to the cells that integrate and regulate life-sustaining functions of the body.

In reality, we have an electrochemical nervous system. When the chemicals change, the messages change, and our brain's performance changes accordingly. When we're in a positive state of mind, it's more likely that we'll operate at the peak of our performance potential. We'll be "in the zone" and feel our best.

Think about how we're always "manifesting." Each thought we have creates an energy flow within and around us. This energy seems to attract its likeness. When we're basically thinking and feeling that "I rock," we exude energy and confidence, which affects our experiences. Our positive thoughts and energy create our reality.

The opposite occurs when we think negative, low-energy thoughts. Then, the outcome tends to knock us down. Negative, selfish and untruthful thoughts quickly yield negative repercussions. Our spirit will know when we're suppressing our conscience, entertaining negative emotions like fear, and becoming the worst version of ourselves. We'll find ourselves feeling trapped and in a state of discontentment.

When this kind of thing happens to us, we need to remember—to *know*—that we're not alone and can break free. The battle is between the mind and spirit, and the truth sets people free.

What happens on the exterior of our life is not as important as what happens inside. Our circumstances are temporary, but our character lasts forever. We don't change ourselves by adjusting our perceptions—we change by believing the truth. If our self-perceptions are wrong, we'll live wrongly— because what we're believing is not true.

So, what are the manifestations of inward energy? Love, joy and peace—also known as the first three inward fruits of the Spirit, as we see in Galatians 5:22-23.

The power of inward energy to change a life

I believe that as we learn to appreciate the One who created "science" through His incomprehensible, indescribable, intelligent design, our hearts will become filled with energy and exceeding gratitude for our Creator. We can win the war and have a genuine, joyful, Holy Spirit-empowered life in Christ. Within me is infinite power, before me is unlimited potential, and around me are boundless opportunities.

We also have assurance that our inheritance—Heaven—is imperishable, undefiled and unfading. We have these assurances in Scripture.

Life on this planet and in our physical bodies can be good, but the next life is unprecedented. There is no comparison. And while we wait for that inheritance, the inward energy that stems from body, mind, and spirit gives us the ability to see that positive change is possible in our lives. It impacts how we see the world and our place in it.

To take it a step further, inward energy helps us look beyond the transient reality of our lives and see a broader range of ideas and solutions by changing the concepts that we choose to focus on. This is the key. It lets us see opportunities instead of obstacles, new roads instead of dead ends, paths to success instead of failure. Energy helps us realize our potential by changing our mindset.

The consequences of not tapping into inward energy

Some people, either out of ignorance or stubbornness, fail to harness the power of inward energy. When this is the case, they suffer from a range of maladies, including unused potential, unnecessary stress and the lack of fulfillment in their lives.

Almost everything in this book spotlights the importance of personal character and integrity, but it takes inward energy, confidence, courage and desire to honestly face our character deficiencies. If we let fear or other factors keep us from taking an honest look at ourselves, we'll end living in a state of denial.

"There are two ways to be fooled," said the famed philosopher Søren Kierkegaard. "One is to believe what isn't true; the other is to refuse to believe what is true."

Well, we certainly don't want to fall into either one of those traps, so we need to understand ourselves—to have a clear conception of how we're made up and how we function. Our thoughts, feelings and behaviors—positive or negative—will have a great influence on the decisions we make and the way we relate to others.

But all of this is rooted in our spiritual center since we're spiritual beings. It's vital to know what our spiritual identity is and the influence that Spirit-given knowledge can have on our psychological and social functioning. When we don't have our inward energy focused on our true Source, we encounter three major "system malfunctions," which I like to call the three I's:

- *Inferiority.* This, of course, is the feeling that "I'm not good enough." We can be tempted, for whatever reasons, to think that other people are worth more than we are. This false conclusion is tied in with low energy and unhappiness.
- *Insecurity.* Some people are filled with fears and doubts about themselves and what may befall them. They can't relax and

experience joy because of their apprehensions, which in turn spawn other symptoms.

- *Inadequacy.* Feelings of overall personal inadequacy, or feelings of inadequacy in certain situations, can possibly make people believe that they'll never be capable of coping with the demands facing them.

The fruit of all of this is guilt, worry and frustration—and part of the remedy is inward energy.

How can we cultivate inward energy?

I think it's apparent by now that inward energy is something that all of us can benefit from. Actually, that understates the case considerably. Inward energy gives us more than just a marginal benefit. We need it on a very profound level.

But how do we channel it into our lives? And how can we cultivate it?

As I see it, the key is to get a grasp on who we are and what we believe—deep down. The biggest part of that task is getting to the place where we realize that we're completely new creations in Christ. We're accepted, secure and significant.

Our decision to follow Christ is the defining moment of our life and will lead to a complete change in who we are. And going right along with that is the fact that we're not saved by how we behave but by what we believe. Of course, if we *are* saved, that can't help but be reflected in our behavior.

Many books have been written on the subject of salvation, but here's my shorthand version of the key points:

- *We need to know who we are—i.e., what our center is.*

- *We need to remove ourselves from being the center of our life and place Christ there instead—which means that we're empowered by His mind, His strength, His peace.*
- *Once we do that, we're set up to live a victorious life, an abundant life, a magnificent life.*

That's the kind of life that gives us the daily, inward energy to persevere and to meet the challenges that life throws our way—and the kind of life that results in unspeakable joy, no matter what we have to endure.

I like the metaphor of faith being like the flange on the inside of a train's wheel. The flange keeps the train on the track when it's rounding curves, and it stabilizes the train under conditions such as heavy winds.

Can people make it in life without faith? Sure! However, when they go around some of life's curves, they're going to fly off the tracks if they don't have that "flange of faith."

We don't want to fall into the trap of thinking that our life foundations are unimportant and insignificant just because we can't see them. Instead, those foundations—faith and the absolute truth of the Bible—are the basis for everything. If we don't get the foundation right, nothing else in our lives will be properly aligned.

It would be hard to overstate how much our lives are affected by our center, our stance and our foundation. As in the game of golf, stance matters in our lives. If my stance is off center, my golf game also will be off center. The best analogy I can think of involves the famous Space Needle landmark in Seattle, Washington. The Space

Needle was built to look like an Olympic torch, and it even had flames coming out of it during the 1962 World's Fair.

This massive, 605-foot tall, very recognizable building has an amazing center of gravity that's only *five feet* above the ground. How is that possible for a building this tall? I learned that the foundation consists of 72 30-foot bolts sunk into 5,600 tons of poured concrete. That's more than 200 trucks full of concrete—the largest pour west of the Mississippi.

Do you have a solid center of gravity? Our stance in this game of life needs to be built on the solid foundation of truth.

A shocking tale

Sorry for the bad pun, but I couldn't resist attaching it to this story about how I got electrocuted.

I was trying to fix my well pump one morning. In my attempt to unstick the relay switch, I stuck a screwdriver into a live contact point. My body took a full dose of 220 volts. This apparently knocked my heart out of rhythm, and I needed a cardioversion treatment and later a heart ablation to restore my normal heartbeat rhythm.

The ablation surgery was simple enough for modern doctors— they ran some wires up my legs to my heart, and then they made a small burn to correct the electrical current flow. Two nurses were by my side, while the electrophysiologist and the cardiologist were in another room managing the procedure on a computer. The nurses' names were Hope and Faith, which was somewhat comforting to me.

Still, a surgery like this is always sobering to the person being operated upon, and I was certainly no exception to that rule. I was somewhat conscious throughout the procedure, so I was able to watch a monitor that showed my heart beating while the wires were moving around and doing their work in my chest.

The medical team performed their task with skill and precision, so I was able to get back to a normal life and resume the jog that I enjoyed every morning. But later I reflected on the fact that just as Hope and Faith helped me change the rhythm of my heart, the lower-case hope and faith help us move our minds and spirits in the right direction.

It was a strange feeling to have 220 volts of electricity coursing through my body. And while I certainly don't recommend getting electrocuted as a way to grow spiritually, I'm glad the experience gave me a new insight or two about hope, faith and inward energy.

Wrapping it all up

I began this chapter describing what happened to me on that hot day in 1979 in Lancaster, South Carolina. Despite the fact that I was young and healthy, I couldn't summon the energy to climb that imposing hill and keep knocking on doors. But my encounter with Jesus in that cluster of trees restored my energy and changed me for life.

I'll always be grateful that on that day, I tapped into a source of enduring energy—and peace and comfort and purpose—that has sustained me for all these decades. My hope is that you'll find that same source of inward energy, which of course is grounded in the Bible as the Word of God and our source of absolute truth.

With that perspective guiding us, we can become and remain spiritually alive. We can be inextinguishable, unstoppable and unable to be destroyed. We'll have the lungs of Earth and the breath of Heaven.

CHAPTER EIGHT

OUTWARD ENERGY

"There is a wonderful mythical law of nature
that the three things we crave most in life—
happiness, freedom, and peace of mind—are
always attained by giving them to someone else."
— *Payton C. Marsh*

This chapter focuses on outcomes—and specifically the kinds of outcomes that derive from the decisions we make and the actions we take.

Central to the discussion is the cause-and-effect principle. This entire concept depends on an undeniable truth: The choices we make produce results—things that are manifested outwardly. Every action (or inaction) yields an outcome. This is the basic cause-and-effect principle that has permeated human existence ever since people figured out that if you shake an apple tree, a piece of fruit might fall into your hands.

Even as babies, we began to figure out that cause and effect could contribute in a mighty way to our happiness. When we were hungry, we'd cry—and milk would miraculously appear. Most children learn this lesson so well that they eventually try ramping up the crying to the level of temper tantrums—at least until their parents intervene and get the condition under control.

The cause-and-effect principle never takes a day off. Everything we do has an impact on our lives. If I were to sit on the couch and eat cheeseburgers and fries for three years (or even three weeks), I'd generate a result or outcome. It may not be an outcome that would be physically healthy or that I'd like to see when I look in the mirror—but it's still an outcome.

This chapter focuses on how our life choices create outcomes that in turn have a dramatic impact on the level of outward energy we have at our disposal. What kind of "outward energy" do we produce—and what do we do with it? That's something we need to be mindful of if we want to harness the power of the Triangle Effect in our lives.

What is outward energy?

One of my friends told me about the "bull sessions" he and his pals used to have when they were in college. Like a lot of young people, they'd sit around discussing some of the major philosophical issues in human existence. One member of this group was a psychology major (he later became a college professor), and one of his favorite refrains was, "Define your terms. What do you mean by that word?" That technique helped keep everyone honest and contributed to clearer discussion.

The words *outward* and *energy* can connote a lot of things—and even more when we combine them. So, for the sake of clarity and (ultimately) usefulness, let's define our terms.

I like to think of *outward* as pointing toward everything outside of our internal life and processes. We're talking here about the results, outcomes and outputs that flow from our decisions and actions. This is the material of our life—our yield, if you will. It's what we create and generate. An analogy might be the way that a computer displays information on the screen. The words, numbers and images on the screen are the visible outcome of the internal CPU processes.

The second word in our chapter title is of course *energy*. This is the drive that propels us forward and is manifested in the productive things that we do.

Now, I hasten to add that this is not a "productivity" book in the sense that the word is used by people in the business world—you know, those hard-driving professionals who want to wring every possible ounce of efficiency out of each day, hour, minute and second.

To be clear, I'm not at all opposed to that kind of literature. I can't count the number of productivity books I've read—and greatly benefitted from, to be sure—over the years. And of course work is a big part of life for many people, so it's no surprise that work factors into our discussion of the Triangle Effect somewhere along the line—and this is the chapter where that happens.

But this chapter is about more than merely helping us achieve efficiency and productivity in our work. It's about living effectively, not just working effectively. It's about being productive in *all* aspects of our lives—and having the right frame of mind about it. In other words, we don't pursue productivity because we want be more efficient producers and sellers of widgets. Instead, by following the principles of the Triangle Effect, we end up being more productive people in virtually every aspect of our lives.

The all-important spiritual dimension

I make no secret about the fact that I bring a spiritual perspective to the writing of this book. In fact, the book is animated by my Christian beliefs. We probe the spiritual dimension of our lives in various parts of *The Triangle Effect*, but I also want to briefly offer a spiritual perspective on it in this particular chapter—since it has an important connection to outward energy.

Now, imagine that we visit an orchard and we pluck a big, red apple from a tree. As we turn it over in our hands, we contemplate how grateful we are for this piece of fruit—and how miraculous the process was that produced it. Maybe we think of Johnny Appleseed as we marvel at how a tiny seed can grow into an amazing tree that can produce more than 500 apples in a single growing season.

I'm sure I'm not the first person to think of this as being a great metaphor for the Christian life. The things that we produce—the various aspects of our *productivity*—flow from the kind of people we are and the kind of character we have.

The Bible repeatedly drives home the point that the fruit of our lives reveals what kind of people we are. In Colossians 1:10-11, believers are exhorted to "live a life worthy of the Lord and please him in every way: bearing fruit in every good work, growing in the knowledge of God, being strengthened with all power according to his glorious might so that you may have great endurance and patience" (NIV).

Another fitting Bible passage is from Galatians 5:22-23: "But the fruit of the Spirit is love, joy, peace, forbearance, kindness, goodness, faithfulness, gentleness and self-control" (NIV).

Actually, the word *fruit* appears in the Bible many times—emphasizing that we should be mindful of the things that our lives bring to fruition. (Did you ever think of how the word *fruit* is so remarkably similar to the word *fruition*?)

We can use the biblical standard to measure all the different outcomes that result from the energy that we direct outward. Life makes sense when we accept our place in God's economy and live from the inside out. The overarching question is, Are we happy with the fruit of our lives?

Medication isn't the answer

Lack of energy has become the number-one complaint in physicians' offices today. People are lethargic, anxious and depressed—resulting in a loss of vitality.

Of course, the "solution" in our pill-oriented culture is to take a prescription. We thus hope to alleviate the symptoms. But if we don't get down to the root cause, we're left grumbling about the side effects of a medication or the high cost of what was supposed to be the latest and greatest miracle drug—with no actual relief in sight.

Medicating symptoms in the absence of addressing their root mental and spiritual causes doesn't energize us. Rather, it leaves us in a state of inaction. What we need to do is achieve the dynamic balancing act found in the physical, mental and spiritual triangle. And we need to be aware that the spiritual aspect of our lives requires greater attention and depth because it's eternal.

Research shows that spiritual energy is stronger than mental energy, and we know that mental energy is much stronger than the physical. This is where the whole "mind over matter" idea originates. It's not a great leap to move from this insight to taking action based on the understanding that power, balance and energy can improve our output in all areas of our lives.

Perceptions of reality

If we want to change virtually anything in our lives, we must first change our reality. Actually, we're not limited as much by our reality as we are by our *perceptions* of our reality.

Of course, there are certain objective facts that we must accept about our lives. We may be broke financially, we may have broken relationships, or we may be physically challenged.

But how we choose to look at those objective facts makes all the difference. It's only when we choose to believe that we live in a universe where challenges can be overcome—and change is possible—that we can summon the energy to make change happen.

I don't mean to suggest that we can make good things happen magically through the power of positive thinking. We can't merely wish away all the obstacles, dead ends and failures in the world.

But it's energizing to see opportunities instead of obstacles and to see pathways instead of dead-ends. We can be motivated to act when we focus on abundance instead of a lack of resources.

It all begins with our ability to see a reality in which anything is possible. We have the power to choose and believe. We have the ability to tap into our enormous potential and live an extraordinarily abundant life. But what's required to make this happen? Sometimes we need to radically change our thinking—and that's what this book is all about.

The Triangle Effect offers three angles for understanding. There's your way and my way—but there's also a third alternative we discover together.

Do you see the glass as half empty or half full? That's a limiting question! Using the Triangle Effect that we've been exploring in this book, we can now imagine a third alternative— such as a pitcher of water right next to that half-full (or half-empty) glass. This free and unique gift of "multiple-perspective angles" allows us the opportunity to assess our thoughts and their impact on our lives along with the output they have.

What's the source of outward energy?

In order to comprehend the big picture, we need to understand where outward energy comes from. I argue that this kind of energy emanates—strangely enough—from something that exists internally: an awareness of truth.

This raises the question of whether there's even such a thing as "objective truth." In our culture today, it's very easy to start to think in relativistic terms. After all, people commonly throw around statements such as "This is *my* truth"—as if perceptions, feelings or opinions are the same as objective reality.

We must resist the cultural tendency to turn truth into something unmoored, unfixed and relative. Otherwise, it's not really *truth*. And truth is essential to getting a firm fix on reality, our identities, and our formulas for living our lives.

It's impossible to arrive at truth without recognizing that God is the author and creator of the universe, that the Bible is His divine word, and that human beings are His spiritual masterpieces.

I find it difficult to believe that these facts are mere figments of the imagination and that we are inconsequential creatures who inhabit the universe by happenstance.

Many people contend that believing in the Bible is for stupid and dependent people because the book is old and therefore outdated. Another argument denigrates science on grounds that it's constantly changing and isn't equipped to answer the philosophical "why" questions.

But if we're truly objective and honest with ourselves, we'll see that the Bible and science are just different vantage points for arriving at truth. Both give us avenues for seeking, encountering and revealing truths about the universe and our place in it.

Sometimes it seems that the Bible is playing offense while science is on defense. Then the roles may be reversed. But both offense and defense are required—just like they would be on a team that's a serious contender for a Super Bowl title.

It's important for us to develop the ability to ascertain truth using whatever means we have at our disposal. If we fail to do that, we'll end up with blind spots that limit our understanding. I appreciate how this insight, attributed to Daniel Goleman, pushes us to try to apprehend truth: "The range of what we think and do is limited by what we fail to notice. And because we fail to notice that we fail to notice, there is little we can do to change until we notice how failing to notice shapes our thoughts and deeds."

It takes effort to pursue truth. As humans, we're tempted to take a shortcut and justify whatever we want to believe. We selectively look for evidence to justify what we believe (or hope) is the truth.

Cognitive bias comes into play here, placing real limits on our ability to think objectively. And ultimately, this affects the decisions and judgments we make about ourselves, others and the universe that surrounds us. The result is that our judgments can be clouded as we gravitate toward perceptions that support our pre-existing attitudes, beliefs and actions.

In our search for truth, we need to look into a mirror and ask, "Who or what am I—really?" We also need to gaze heavenward and give serious thought to whether the God of the Bible really exists. I think it's logical to conclude that no human being could design the universe, or even just the universe between our ears—not to mention making it all work in harmony.

Only a thorough understanding of these issues can generate the kind of outward energy that we need for effective living.

How choices propel us forward

Philosophers have thought and written deeply about "free will" for many centuries. Starting with the ancient Greeks (e.g., Plato and Aristotle) and continuing on through the ages, philosophers have explored the various dimensions of human agency—the ability to make choices. And if some of the greatest thinkers in world history have cared about free will, maybe we should, too.

We have the power to choose. We can choose to act with kindness and compassion, or we can choose enormous evil. We can choose to be thoughtful and reflective in our life decisions, or we can simply float down the river of life, directed by currents beyond our control.

We can choose to get in sync with our Creator, or we can choose to ignore God's design for living.

It's important to realize, however, that all of these choices have a direct impact on how much outward energy is manifested in our lives.

Consider these pairings:

- *Love | Hate*
- *Act | Procrastinate*
- *Persevere | Quit*

Only one word in each pair results in positive energy that propels us forward. This kind of choice is a gift, and when harnessed properly, it can be a tremendous force in our lives.

But if good choices help us keep our momentum going, poor choices can arrest our forward progress. We can all come up with examples of times when we made a bad decision, found ourselves stymied, and paid a hefty price.

Well, life on Planet Earth takes place in a linear fashion. We don't have the power to go back and revise the past. But we can strive to apply wisdom in all the choices we make from now on.

From time to time, we should stop and take inventory in regard to how our choices are impacting us. Are they helping us thrive, or are they holding us back? If we want to have the energy we need for successful living, we can't neglect the power of choice.

The choice is ours—a barren life rooted in anger, bitterness and resentment, or a productive, fruitful life grounded in freedom, forgiveness and a God-centered belief system. When we cultivate awareness of how our choices amplify our outward energy, we become capable of more than we ever thought possible.

What happens when we miss the mark

If we don't tap into outward energy, we can suffer negative consequences. What might they be? Let's take inventory.

For starters, we'll exist in what I call a "weak state of being." How could it be otherwise, right? If we're not animated by energy, we might struggle to get off the couch. Our lack of purpose, drive and motivation will be reflected in the things that we fail to accomplish in our personal and professional lives. We become our own worst enemy—the person we don't want to be.

If we're not careful, all of that can snowball into what I call a "DIM" life. That is, our minds can end up being filled with delusions, illusions and misperceptions. This crowds out the good stuff, and of course that's not the head space we want to be in. Instead, we want outward energy to do its work in keeping us plugged in, on task and motivated.

I don't mean to suggest that we'll always be completely "pumped up," taking the tiger by its tail. It's inevitable that we'll have moments when we're just not feeling the energy vibe. But when we sustain outward energy over the long haul, our lives are more productive, rewarding and meaningful.

Before we leave this section, let's also consider one more downside to moving through life without a sufficient reserve of outward energy.

I firmly believe that there's a whole constellation of negatives that permeate a life that isn't animated by energy. In keeping with the Triangle Effect's grouping of elements into three, we can organize these negatives thusly:

- *We're in danger of feeling inferior, insecure and inadequate.*
- *Our lives may be dominated by worry, doubt and fear—as well as frustrations, hostility and fantasy.*
- *We perceive that life is filled not with paths forward but with roadblocks, obstacles and dead ends.*

This reminds me of a mini essay that I encountered some years ago and have kept in my files ever since. Attributed to an unknown author, the piece is called "The Loser." It reviews a number of counterproductive attitudes that infect the attitudes of the real losers in life, and it concludes with these words:

> *A loser specializes in complaints, gripes, arguments, excuses, and assumptions. He loses jobs, friends, opportunities, and loved ones.*
>
> *A loser says that life is a rotten deal, and he spends all his time trying to prove it. He's the gloomiest, most cynical, suspicious defeatist in the world.*
>
> *A loser is depressed, discouraged, afraid, and lonely. He doesn't admit it, but he needs many things; and, above all, he needs enlightenment, understanding and love.*

What a waste of time, talent and resources to go through life in such a counterproductive mental state. The cultivation of outward energy is one of the antidotes.

Generating the energy

Let's begin this section by contemplating an appliance that we all have in our homes—the refrigerator. Things have changed since, as a lad, I got home from school and headed to the fridge for a snack. These days, some of the models are pretty fancy. They feature snazzy LED lighting, dispensers for water and ice, computer displays on the doors—and some models will even order groceries automatically when the stock of ice cream gets low!

What an amazing appliance the old "icebox" has turned out to be. However, suppose that someone accidentally unplugged the new refrigerator. Would it still be a refrigerator, by definition? Yes, of course. But would it work the way it was designed? Of course not.

Now, let's apply a similar perspective to our lives. If we aren't plugged in, so to speak, are we functioning the way we should? Are we performing at a high level? Are we generating the kind of energy that's required for us to live our best lives? Clearly, the answer would be no.

A refrigerator gets plugged into a wall and *uses* energy from an electrical circuit. In contrast, a person plugs into God's "circuitry" and *generates* energy.

Now, if we depend for outward energy on a false or superficial kind of circuitry—rather than that which comes from divine revelation and biblical wisdom—we are deluding ourselves.

The Bible teaches us that there is a God—and it's not us. Personally, I'm very grateful there's someone far wiser and more competent who is running the show. If the Creator, Supreme Being or Author of the Universe is in control, then I'm not—and that's a very freeing perspective.

Once we understand how God is in charge, we can see how much hubris it takes to build self-centered lives, to believe that our own resources are sufficient to the needs of the day, and to construct monuments to our own glory. The likely outcome of such conceits: the collapse of our little house of cards.

The bottom line is that if we live to gratify our own desires, we'll end up running on fumes.

But if we're willing to tap into God's design for our lives, we'll have all the outward energy we need.

The need to surrender

How do we tap into the aforementioned energy that comes from God's design?

First, we have to be willing to embrace it. Many times, we reach this point only when we hit rock bottom or arrive at the end of our proverbial rope. *That's* when we begin to understand that our human designs don't cut it—that we need to turn our goals, plans and lives over to God.

The key concept here is surrender. In surrendering to God, we let go of our selfishness. We usher in a revolution of the soul, in which we take ourselves out of the center of the universe and place God there.

In the last chapter, I related my personal story about surrendering my fragile self to Jesus on that brutally hot afternoon in Lancaster, South Carolina. One thing I learned was that losing leads to finding. Until I cut the ropes that tethered me to my own ideas of self-determination, I couldn't discover the much better way that God offered me. Amazingly, the one act of the will that produces an abundance of outward energy is surrender—which actually fuels our vitality.

Now, surrendering is a difficult concept for most people. The term has mostly negative connotations in our culture—it conjures up images of wartime defeat and perhaps even humiliation. But when we think of the vast gulf between our humble lives and the immense superiority of our Creator—a gulf that we can't even begin to comprehend—it makes perfect sense for us to embrace the concept of surrender. This is how we find the way forward.

There are three main barriers that block our total surrender to God: worry, pride and confusion. This is the battleground where our self-centered nature resists what we know is right. But somewhere along the line, we have to face the truth about ourselves. We are all pitiful actors who wear false masks and play fake roles.

Yet if we're truly honest with ourselves, somewhere in our innermost being is a desire to know and please God. There's a need, in the depths of my soul, to know God in a very personal way and to feel His love. When I cultivate that, I gain the inner freedom to live a magnificent, extraordinary and abundant life.

It's important to note that when we decide to live by God's

precepts, the point isn't to align with a particular church, adopt a certain dogma or take a specific stance on this or that moral issue—although we certainly may be led to action along those lines. Neither are we motivated by fear of eternal damnation.

Instead, we are attracted by the idea of grace, the promise of forgiveness, and the prospect of living a better, more-fulfilling life. It's a positive motivation, not one that's grounded in fear and negativity. That's why following God generates energy from the inside out.

Victory over the darkness

Those who decide to take the journey would do well to remember that there's a constant, daily struggle between our spiritual and human natures. Sometimes, in my weak, frail and sin- prone state, I feel like a slave who is bound to fail in front of every temptation and trial that comes my way.

But thankfully, victory over the darkness is possible. Here are three things you can put on a 3x5 index card and carry with you in your heart. There is...

- *no depth from which God cannot lift us.*
- *no sorrow in which He cannot comfort us.*
- *no sin beyond His pardon and forgiveness.*

What I do is simply ask the Holy Spirit to show me how to honestly deal with the evil that is present in me. To me, it doesn't matter where it came from, how it originated or how it got into my mind. All I know is that it is there, that I don't want it to control me, and that I need to be freed from it.

Here are three simple absolutes that the Bible teaches us. They're easy to understand with childlike faith.

- *We are all sinners—no one is innocent.*

- *Our sins make us slaves. In other words, we're in a state of hopeless bondage.*
- *A plan was devised for our freedom—and the plan consists of believing rather than doing.*

You may be thinking that this all makes sense in your mind—but you wonder how it becomes a reality in your life.

First, we have to apprehend and internalize the fact we are made in God's image. That makes every one of us very special—even miraculous. Then we should cultivate awareness of the fact that we often fail to be what we should be because we can't stop being what we think we are.

Outward energy is key here. With each new day, we receive a free gift of 86,400 seconds.

Then we have the power to choose how to spend each second. This book is all about seeing from a different angle the marvelous adventure of being a magnificently, divinely and uniquely designed product of God's creation. When we believe, surrender and abide, our life's story will move from darkness to light.

Life is so precious. Time is irreplaceable. Each day is a gift. Yesterday is gone, and tomorrow has not yet arrived. The legendary basketball coach John Wooden, winner of 10

NCAA national championships, learned a lesson from his father, Joshua Wooden, that he went on to teach to his players: "Make each day your masterpiece." That's powerful advice. If we make each day our masterpiece, how much would that change the story of our lives?

The ultimate destination

As we wrap up this chapter, let's make sure we have a firm handle on what outward energy is and how it can be manifested in our lives.

I think of it this way: If we're living in harmony with God's design, we'll be enabled, empowered and encouraged to channel energy in and through our lives. We won't be passive bystanders watching life go by all around us. Instead, we'll be people who have the energy to move, to resolve, to take action—so that we're fully engaged in the work that God would have us do on this planet. We've all been endowed with gifts that we can use to bless the world. Outward energy gives us the capacity to deploy them.

St. Francis of Assisi said, "It is through giving that we receive." I believe we energize, maximize and enjoy our life more when we choose to be a giver of life in our words, deeds and resources.

A good analogy for elaborating on outward energy involves a story I heard about the tale of two legendary and historically important bodies of water—the Sea of Galilee and the Dead Sea.

The Sea of Galilee has a large variety of fish and plant life. The area around the sea is filled with birds, rich soil, resorts, farms, commerce, tourism and lush vineyards. In stark contrast is the Dead Sea, which has no plant life and no fish.

The first body of water gives life and flourishes. The second is lifeless. What's interesting, though, is that both seas are fed by the Jordan River. The difference is that the Jordan *flows through* the Sea of Galilee before its water continues its journey down the river. But eventually the Jordan feeds into the Dead Sea, which has no outlet—not to mention extraordinarily high salt content. As a result, the water stagnates.

The tale of the two seas can be a metaphor for life. Think in terms of relationships and how we deal with what we own. Do we choose gratefulness and thankfulness and then share liberally—letting blessings flow through us as the Jordan River flows through the Sea of Galilee? Or do choose to hoard our gifts? In the latter case, the flow of outward energy stops, and we become stagnant. The level of outward energy in our lives depends on whether we want to be like the Sea of Galilee or the Dead Sea.

But as I've tried to make clear in this chapter, energy comes from God. He's the one who fuels the purpose, movement and vitality of our lives. We don't just drift along and then magically become fountains of world-blessing productivity. We pursue God, and then we're energized to do what He'd have us do in our lives.

I've always found Mother Teresa to be an inspiring example of outward energy. This diminutive nun was not particularly strong in a physical sense. However, when we observe and admire the incredible work she did among the some of the most destitute people in the world, we can clearly see that her outward energy was wildly disproportional to her physical size. That's because her actions were inspired and sustained by her inner spiritual life.

May we all aspire to generate even a fraction of the outward energy that Mother Teresa blessed the world with.

CHAPTER NINE

UPWARD ENERGY

> "Oh, the utter extravagance of his work in us who
> trust him—endless energy, boundless strength!"
> —*Ephesians 1:19 (MSG)*

This is the ninth and final chapter of *The Triangle Effect*. I think we've saved the best for last.

By now, I hope you're looking differently at some of the things in your life—and also that this new perspective carries over to the way you relate to and value the people around you.

I also like to think that since you've read this far, you've gained a few insights about yourself and why you "do life" the way you do. This process of understanding can give us valuable clues about why we thrive and flourish in certain situations—and why we sometimes languish and fall short in others. Of course, these insights and clues help us figure out how to live, work and play more effectively.

The most important thing

In the previous two chapters, we've talked about inward and outward energy. Now we turn our attention to upward energy. What does this term signify and imply?

It's pretty simple. We're talking about the kind of energy that's connected to having a personal relationship with God—by locating ourselves in His story of mankind. When we're aligned vertically by loving and following God, we'll also find that our lives also are aligned horizontally—that is, we'll have better relationships with the people around us. Where better to learn patience, kindness and forgiveness than in our relationships with others?

There is a Triangle Effect advantage of companionship. In Ecclesiastes 4:12, we read: "A person standing alone can be attacked and defeated, but two can stand back-to-back and conquer. Three are even better, for a triple-braided cord is not easily broken" (NIV).

It might seem like an odd connection, but think for a moment about the Christian faith, logos and symbols. In an era of widespread commercialism, we've come to instantly recognize logos. People around the world associate a certain "swoosh" (meaning victory) with athleticism—even if the word Nike isn't attached to it. The Apple logo signifies knowledge and represents one of the world's most profitable technology companies.

One of my personal favorites is the Infiniti car symbol, which represents performance without limitations. This symbol encourages us to step forward and to try, even when everyday logic may be telling us that victory is beyond our physical ability or means. The point in the middle of the symbol shows the apex of sophistication. Aim high! Think big! Go bold!

But when we think about our faith in Jesus Christ, we have the most unique and powerful symbol in human history—the cross. When Jesus was crucified more than 2,000 years ago, the cross represented pain, humiliation and death. But thanks to the Resurrection, the meaning of this symbol has been transformed. Now we understand it to mean sacrificial love, salvation and victory over death.

Upward energy rarely comes to us in a neat package. It's earned in pieces and life lessons that flow through moments of confusion and suffering as well as decades of relationships. No amount of researching, reading or Googling will bring us exhaustive knowledge of ourselves and the universe. There will always be the question of what happens to us when we die.

Death is a potentially frightening subject that most people don't like to talk about. I know this very well from 40-plus years of selling life insurance and planning and settling estates.

However, we know that death is inevitable. It's the only real constant. I *am* going to die. I don't know when, and I don't know how, but I do know for sure that I will die at some point.

Providentially, the Bible teaches us that while Jesus predicted His own future, talked about death and even contemplated His own death, He had victory over death after three days in the grave—giving us a profound sense of hope. I can't explain it, but I know there's Someone in my life who is the source of this thought—and that assurance makes me feel whole.

Today, we can't assume that we have widespread biblical literacy in our society. Many people have no idea what the story of Jesus is all about. So let me spell it out here at the start of the chapter—in hopes that everything that follows will make sense.

The Holy Bible gives us reliable information about the life, death and resurrection of Jesus. This is the gospel—the "good news." The story has generated an untold number of historical and theological works over the years, but the essence of it is that God's son, Jesus, was born in human form, was put to death on the cross for the sins of humankind, and was resurrected on the third day—showing the power of God over sin and death and giving us the promise of eternal life with Him if we only believe and follow.

The Bible contains a lot more material, of course—Old Testament stories, Psalms, Proverbs and instructional letters to the early church. But by far the most important message of the Bible is God's offer of salvation and eternal life through Jesus. This is the framework for our focus in this chapter on upward energy—the kind of animating life energy that can come only from living in harmony with our Creator.

Full vitality in life

The Bible teaches that God's grace is sufficient for us and that his power is made perfect in our weakness. This is manifested in the transformative paradigm of upward energy.

But we have to be careful not to get the wrong idea here. The kind of upward energy I'm talking about isn't to be equated with an "energy drink" that will improve our athletic prowess.

Rather, we can think of upward energy as a source of strength and inspiration as we reach our full potential and live the way God intended. The power of upward energy is the divine authority and vitality that God pours into the life of every one of his children in order that we might live a fruitful life in full abundance. We recognize this by the love, compassion and wisdom that pour out of us like a fresh mountain stream.

I believe that when we get to the end of what we can make of ourselves, we're only at the beginning of what the Holy Spirit can do in terms of energizing our bodies, enlightening our minds and igniting the passions of our hearts. We are poised to move forward and start realizing the potential that God has for us. Upward energy is experienced when we allow the Holy Spirit to nudge us, prod us, push us, mold us, remake us and fashion us into the fullness of our potential. We'll be fully alive on the inside and will have complete freedom to live in hope, love and joy.

One of my personal tendencies (or flaws, if you will) is that I try to "domesticate" God. I'm tempted to figure out ways of harnessing his power for my own projects and priorities. I seem to think I can reduce God to a factor that facilitates my plans. I then find that I end up in motion but without any meaningful sense of direction. Unfortunately, I have learned this same lesson over and over in my life—or maybe I haven't learned it that well after all. The bottom line is that God cannot be fit into my plans; I must fit into his. God is not an ATM, an unlimited credit card or my personal Santa Claus.

Accessing upward energy

Where does upward energy originate? It's not something we can conjure up on our own. It's not a product of gritting our teeth and redoubling our human efforts. Instead, the source of upward energy is God Himself. This kind of energy permeates our lives and reflects the glory of our Creator and the fact that He inhabits our heart, soul and mind.

In Ephesians 2:8-10, we read: "God saved you by his grace when you believed. And you can't take credit for this; it is a gift from God. Salvation is not a reward for the good things we have done, so none of us can boast about it. For we are God's masterpiece. He has created us anew in Christ Jesus, so we can do the good things he planned for us long ago" (NLT).

The key words in our context here are "we can do the good things he planned for us." God calls us to action, and action requires effort, and effort requires energy—so you can see how important it is to access this source of upward energy.

We often hear athletes talk about "digging deep" in competition, and that's great—in the athletic arena. But again, the kind of energy we're focusing on in this chapter doesn't depend on human efforts. Instead, it's a supernatural strength that arises from the God who not only created us but also dwells within us. This is the kind of energy that sustains us throughout our entire lives and whatever difficulties we happen to be going through. Thanks to upward energy, we have the wherewithal to keep moving forward.

The beginning of this chapter featured a verse from Ephesians 1:19: "Oh, the utter extravagance of his work in us who trust him—endless energy, boundless strength!" (MSG).

This is the birthright of believers, and it would be a shame if we didn't take full advantage of it.

I think there's also a poetic dimension to the concept of upward energy. For example, contemplate how we're energized by the beauty of a sunset, the grandeur of a snow-capped mountain range, and the awesomeness of a star-filled sky. Natural beauty is one of the mechanisms that God uses to energize us. We can find this kind of inspiration and energy whenever we like.

Three levels of being

The Triangle Effect is about seeing things from different perspectives and going deep into our innermost being. This takes effort and concentration, and it might be difficult for some people at first.

But it gets easier as we work on it. Imagine a rocket ship taking off from Cape Canaveral. It takes an enormous amount of energy to get off the ground—you've seen video of the billowing steam clouds—and then to break through the force of Earth's gravity. Once that point has been reached, however, traveling through space is much easier.

Similarly, the going is easier when we break free of the distractions in our lives—what we could think of as "life gravity" in this metaphor. Gravity can take a lot of forms, and we need to be attentive to many of them, for sure—getting the kids to school or practice, paying the bills, and making certain that we have adequate insurance coverage.

But somehow, we have to find a way to break free of the stuff of daily life and access the deep well within us. Like a tree that sends its roots deep in the ground, we must learn to tap into the glorious energy and power that God makes available to us. As Jesus is quoted as saying in John 7:37-38: "If anyone thirsts, let him come to me and drink. Rivers of living water will brim and spill out of the depths of anyone who believes in me this way, just as the Scripture says" (MSG).

As we drill down into the depths of our being, let's consider three levels of awareness and engagement.

Level 1. At this level of awareness and being, we're dealing with the superficial and shallow.

Our fleeting thoughts careen from one distraction to the next. You've probably noticed this in your own life: Your mind can wander into a fluttering array of random, disconnected thoughts that lead nowhere. This kind of focus is similar to random surfing on the Internet. You can fool around and burn a lot of time there. Of course, we may think we're getting smarter by spending hours on the Internet, but we're actually cultivating distraction and ignorance. The person at Level 1 is not hitting on all cylinders either intellectually or relationally. When I fall into this trap, I find that I have no margin in my life—the distractions are just too great.

Level 2. This level represents progress over the first one, but we're still stuck in middle-ground thoughts, concerns and aspirations. We're focused on things like our health, our money and our relationships. Make no mistake—these are good things to be focused on! We shouldn't neglect them. But there's a still-higher level of awareness and being.

Level 3. This is where we encounter the depths of our being—the innermost place, the core of our life. This space is accessible only by God, not by other human beings. It's where we hold our deepest yearnings related to faith, hope and love. A biblical phrase that might apply here is "the Holy of Holies." My hope is that you'll build greater awareness of this deep inner life...and encounter your Creator there.

One of the challenges in life is to move from the pull and superficiality of level 1 all the way to level 3, where we have a deep and abiding relationship with God. This is an important aspect of cultivating upward energy.

Understanding our uniqueness

I have a purpose in life, and you do, too—but our purposes are different. I have gifts, but they're not your gifts. I have dreams, but they're not your dreams. You and I probably don't resemble each other physically. Has there ever been another person with exactly your eyes, your hair, your nose? Probably not—unless, perhaps, you're an identical twin.

The point, of course, is that we're all unique. There's no such thing as "one size fits all" when it comes to our journeys through life. However, one thing we do have in common is the ability to draw on upward energy to live more effectively and with a greater sense of purpose. In the previous section, we touched on the fact that we need to drill down into our innermost being to truly understand who we are. But we don't have to scale a mountain, sit on a yoga mat and contemplate our existence for days at a time to access these insights.

Let me suggest one practical way of moving forward with this project—and that's to take one of the many online tests that can help you identify your unique characteristics. The one that I've used the most is the popular assessment from the VIA Institute on Character. I recommended this in chapter 2, when we were discussing goals. It applies here as well.

If you take VIA's free, 10-minute assessment, you'll probably have a greater ability to appreciate and ignite your positive character strengths—and be aware of your weaker ones, so that you can work on them. Ultimately, this kind of activity builds awareness that can help us tap into upward energy in our own unique ways.

For the reader who wants to go to an advanced level of spiritual depth, I recommend taking the sacred pathways assessment by Gary Thomas. This resource will help you understand the different ways people connect with God. We all have been designed with unique spiritual gifts and temperaments. Thomas shows nine different pathways. Some people connect with God outside in nature, some connect while caring for people in need, some connect where spiritual warfare and confrontation are concerned, and some connect better in contemplative meditation or intellectual study. I find this to be a very insightful perspective.

I believe that when we understand our own uniqueness, we can then appreciate the uniqueness of others. Find your path and incorporate it into your life, and you'll increase your upward energy. Try it for three days, and you'll be amazed. Try it for three weeks, and you'll be changed. In three months, you'll be transformed.

God as the source

Apart from God, we won't be able to tap into the kind of upward energy under consideration in this chapter. That's because God is the source of this energy. Without God, there would be little point in focusing our attention "upward."

Within that context, we can reflect on the limits of our own efforts in contrast to the energy that God can provide. Remember that God is *omnipotent*—which is a fancy word for all- powerful. God is *omniscient*—all-knowing. And God is *omnipresent*, meaning that means that he is both eternal and ever-present in every moment of history and thus in every moment of our lives. When we reach the limits of what we can accomplish in our human frailty, we are at only the beginning of what God can do through us.

God is always available, always attentive and always interested in our lives. He gives us his full love, compassion and grace. That's nothing short of astonishing. If we could comprehend that more fully, our lives would change dramatically.

Upward energy energizes, enlightens and empowers us as we move forward into our full potential—the full potential of our love, obedience and devotion.

Many times in life, I've tried to define and reach my full potential using my own human resources. I almost always fail, which inevitably leads to disappointment, discouragement and perhaps even depression. The real key to reaching our full potential lies in trusting God to help us become our best.

Here are three important questions to ask God:

- *What do you want me to do?*
- *When and how do you want me to act?*
- *How can I best represent you today?*

When we open up to upward energy, God will give us guidance and direction—even though sometimes it may not take the form we expect. But only God sees the beginning as well as the ending of our life. Only God knows where we are on his timetable of development. Only God knows the full set of plans he has established for us.

Reflecting God's light

I have distinct memories about my father singing a popular song about the moon when I was a child. Perhaps we'd be camping, or we'd be playing golf until the sun went down. But when that giant orb illuminated the dark, my dad would sing, *Oh Mister Moon, moon bright and shining moon, won't you please shine down on me.*

The moon is probably the first celestial object that children notice in the night sky. Later, in school, we learn how this big rock is orbiting the earth at the same time that the Earth is orbiting the sun. We also learn about the moon's rhythms, phases and monthly cycles, all of which help form a harmonious Triangle Effect relationship. The moon's gravitational pull is the key to making our planet livable by moderating the degree of wobble in the earth's axial tilt. It's all beautifully choreographed.

But what we want to recognize is that the moon doesn't have energy of its own like the sun does. Instead, it simply reflects the sun's light. This big, beautiful object in the sky seems perfectly content to reflect light from a far-greater source.

This is a pretty good analogy for how we as humans are designed to reflect the light and glory of God in our lives. When we surrender to a higher power than ourselves—indeed, the greatest power in the universe—miracles seem to happen. When we quiet ourselves, we resonate in harmony with God's voice, and we are no longer merely witnesses of God's power—we also are empowered by the upward energy that He provides for us.

To experience the transformation that we were designed for, we must let God change our perspective, which in turn will help us see what He sees. I like to think of God as a kind of invisible hand, with me being a glove that is filled and operated by the hand. I need to allow my glove to be filled by the divine hand so that I can function as I was designed to.

Momentarily encountering the power of God is one thing. However, to be established or firmly rooted in that power is another thing entirely. The word "righteousness" refers to the character of God, which is manifested in purity, boldness, courage, faithfulness, love, mercy and many more attributes. When attributes such as those are established in our lives, we are enveloped in upward energy. That's real power, balance and energy—the very practical Triangle Effect where and when we need it. Like the moon, we reflect a greater light.

Life challenges and upward energy

Have you ever felt defeated, trapped in bondage and maybe even worthless? Hitting rock bottom, with no energy to get moving, actually can be a good thing. Why? Because when our sense of self-sufficiency is reduced to zero, that's when we realize for certain that we are not God—and never will be. It's at this point of abject personal weakness that we have the opportunity to make radical changes and experience upward energy.

Let's probe a little deeper. When we survey our lives, we see many pitfalls, problems and challenges. We typically learn at a young age that life can come at us with a stick and a club. In those hard moments, it's not uncommon to hear someone say, "Man, I really need some help from the Man Upstairs."

God seems to be on the mind of many people, even if they aren't thinking about him in strictly theological terms. According to the Gallup polling organization, more than 90% of Americans believe in God. The vast majority say their beliefs are very important to them and have a large effect on their lives—yet I suspect that many of these people aren't really on intimate terms with God.

I want to make the argument that our personal, caring God is with us even when the world is chaotic, illogical and frightening. Here's an example of that from my own life.

Back in 1982, when I was 23, I was really struggling to get by financially and to provide for my wife and new daughter. I remember collecting some pennies from a glass jar, putting them in paper rolls, and using this form of legal tender to buy a little gas so I could get to work. My sales commissions were always up and down, and there were many months when I'd need to get a loan from a local bank just to pay my bills.

Driving home one evening, just when I thought things couldn't get much worse financially, the muffler fell off my sleek, black 1978 Monte Carlo. Truthfully, I couldn't really afford this nice car with a T-Top—it was my "fake it until you make it" vehicle.

But since I was low on money and had no other way to get the muffler fixed, I was forced to use a Sears credit card that I received when I graduated from college. While waiting for the car to be repaired at Sears, I met a local Allstate insurance agent at her kiosk in the store. That chance meeting led to an amazing and fulfilling career for me with Allstate—one that provided very well for the growing family that 40 years ago I had been struggling to support. I see this as evidence that God is with us even in dark and desperate times.

Of course, sometimes the endings aren't quite so happy. We all experience this. Random accidents, events and medical diagnoses can turn our lives upside down. Yet I believe that God remains in full control of the universe that seems so random and chaotic from our limited human perspective. This may be counterintuitive, but when we feel that we have things totally under control, that's when we could very well be the most *out* of control.

More broadly, God never intended for us to merely cope with life. His design is for our lives to be animated by the upward energy he generously makes available to us. Many believers make the mistake of asking God to help them rather than just yielding to his upward energy so that he can live in and through them. God's supernatural power fills us and enables us to be victorious over all the many circumstances and pressures we face.

Whatever way the winds are blowing, however, we should never feel lost or insignificant. We should always feel that we have hope because God is our refuge and strength—our source of upward energy.

Inspiration from the 3x5 notecards

This world that we live in can certainly pull us in many directions, so it's always important to have a mission or purpose statement to keep our "GPS life system" plugged in. I'd like to give another personal example—this time stemming from a rough patch that I recently had to navigate. This story takes us on an excursion to Florida, where my father resided.

After my father had his 90th birthday, he started to experience failing health. At the same time, his wife had a severe case of "angry Alzheimer's." I figured this would be a good time for me to drive to Florida, surprise him with a visit, and help him do video chats with a new great- grandson named in his honor. I was in a position to miss some work, and I had a new set of wheels, so I figured I'd be having a fun road trip.

Well, things got out of hand very quickly. I had to take my father to the hospital for treatment of a heart infection, kidney failure and a host of other issues. I was running to the hospital early every morning to meet with his various doctors, and then I'd go back to his home to care for his wife, go to the store, deal with the bank, explore home-healthcare options, and so on. I ended up staying on this hamster wheel for six long months.

My dad had always been on top of everything, so the situation felt really out of control. Everything was now up to me—and I'd always had enough trouble running my own life.

I was very thankful that my sister showed up to help, but we still had our hands full. The result was that I fell out of the rhythm and routine that had served me well for the past 40 years.

Without my coffee, reading time and workout, I wasn't even close to being "in the zone," as they say.

As I worked through this difficult time, I began to understand the concept of *essentialism*, and I pared away anything in my mind that didn't need to be there. With no time to read and relax, I needed a way to stay focused on what was critically important. I also needed to stay in touch with my Creator.

My solution was to look through the hundreds of 3x5 index cards that I had collected over the years—and then to grab a stack that I could keep in my pocket and read from time to time.

Ten of my favorite cards from this period are presented in the next section.

The lifeline of 3x5 cards

What sustained me through those long and difficult months in Florida was my "greatest hits" collection of index cards. I'll share some of them here. Many of these are paraphrased from passages I've encountered in books and articles over the years.

- *This is the beginning of a new day. I have been given this day to use as I will. What I do today is important because I am*

exchanging a whole day of my life for it. When tomorrow comes,
this day will be gone forever, leaving in its place whatever I have
traded for it.

Abraham Lincoln said, "The best thing about the future is that it only comes only one day at a time." As we encounter those days, it can be helpful to think in terms of *investing* our time instead of *spending* our time.

A simple technique for doing this is to write down, every morning, three things we *must* accomplish before the day is done. We put these "A priority" items on an index card. Then we write down three things we *want* to accomplish after the first three are done—"B priority" items. Finally, we can write down three things that it would be *nice* to get done if time allows or they can be worked in throughout the day—these are "C priority." Refer back to the index card throughout the day. The goal is to make each day count.

- *My mission is to do what is acceptable to you, God. Align me with your will, and help me be in full harmony with other people, the universe and you. May I maintain a positive, peaceful attitude in everything I do.*

A meditation like this helps me do what a golfer does—maintain a good grip. A poor grip can lead to all sorts of problems—in a golf swing as well as in life. In a similar vein, the things that grip our time, energy and attention will have a profound impact on what we accomplish. Therefore, it's important to start each day by focusing on our personal mission, philosophy or creed. If you don't already have a strong personal mission statement, you should write one. I recommend something very simple and easy to remember.

- *My thinking and my attitudes are reflected in a calm and cheerful disposition. I act and feel friendly toward others. I strive to be tolerant of other people and their shortcomings and mistakes. I view people in the most favorable light possible.*

The only thing we can do on a daily basis is play one note at a time. "Stop, look, go" is what we teach our children about crossing a street. The same approach applies in our lives. We must slow down, think and make good choices. The remarkable thing is that we can choose every day what kind of attitude to adopt. We can't change the past, nor can we change other people and the way they act. However, we can choose to be calm, positive and cheerful—and enjoy the energy that these attributes produce.

- *I try to smile as often as possible. I respond in a calm and intelligent manner without alarm, no matter what the situation. If I cannot control a situation, I try always to react in a positive manner—even to negative facts and occurrences.*

There is physiological evidence that smiling has significant consequences. This is even truer of laughter. There's a feedback loop here. The more we smile and laugh, the better we feel—and the more inclined we are to keep the cycle going. Humor and laughter can even have medicinal and healing effects.

- *God, if you are in control, then I must lose control, because as long as I am in control, I am really out of control. God, be merciful to me a sinner.*

It's human nature to think that we're in control—but we're not. And it's a very liberating feeling when we realize that after surrendering control to Jesus Christ, we have become spiritually alive. I believe that we are spiritual beings who have a human experience—rather than human beings who have a spiritual experience. We were made in God's image, and that spiritual nature is part of our original design.

- *Jesus, I believe you died for me and that your precious blood will cleanse me from all my sins—past, present and future. By faith, I receive you, Jesus, into my heart as my Lord and Savior, trusting you for the salvation of my soul.*

I used this card to remind me of my commitment. "Trust" is a key word on that index card. When we trust God, we stop trusting in all the inferior motivations that can govern our lives—ego, pride, vanity. Those things drain our lives of purpose and vitality. But when we trust God and understand that we are created in his image, we become animated and empowered by upward energy.

- *I rest in your mercy and faithfulness. I recognize that I cannot live the Christian life in my own strength or out of my own resources. I now give up my self-sufficiency and hereby commit my life unconditionally into your hands, and I choose to allow you to live your life through me.*

If we rely on the Lord's strength, the pressure's off. We don't have to do everything in our own power. Instead, God works through us. Ecclesiastes 10:10 presents a helpful way of looking at this: "Using a dull ax requires great strength, so sharpen the blade" (NLT). Abraham Lincoln reportedly said, "If I had six hours to chop down a tree, I'd spend the first four hours sharpening the axe." This index card gave me a daily reminder that I should rely on God's strength, not my own.

- *Father, Author of the universe, Creator God, help me to humble myself before you. Save me from the pride and arrogance that cuts me off from your hand of blessing. Teach me to walk softly today before you and never lose sight of your greatness and my need.*

The "theme of three" has served us well throughout *The Triangle Effect*, but when we reflect on the attributes of God, we need a far-greater number. Volumes have been written on this, but here's my countdown of nine cards that I often carry with me on days when I know I'll be challenged:

#9 God is love—benevolent and good. His ultimate purpose is to favor us and draw us into a loving relationship with him. He made the ultimate sacrifice to make this relationship possible. All His actions toward us are motivated by this love.

#8 God is all-knowing. He sees the beginning and the end. He is the ultimate source of all knowledge and truth. He knew us before time began and when we were being formed in the womb.

#7 God is personal. He is not a far-off, disembodied being. He relates to us on a personal level.

#6 God is three in one—Father, Son and Holy Spirit. He is knowable in all dimensions as He lives within us.

#5 God is infinite. He is everywhere. He cannot be measured or understood by human minds. He is the beginning and the end. He is the cause of all things.

#4 God is immanent. We can sense his presence all around us. He is with us in ways we do not understand. He is above all things, and at the same time, He is in all things, sustaining the entire universe.

#3 God is all-powerful. He is sovereign. He rules over the entire creation and is attentive to all details. All things are under His control, and all history is under His authority.

 # 2 God is transcendent. He is from another world outside our own. He is beyond our thinking and imagination. He cannot be represented by anything in our world. He is above all.

#1 God is holy. There is nothing evil in Him. He is compared to pure light, which darkness cannot overcome. Holiness is his greatest and all-encompassing attribute. He is Holy in everything He is and does.

Perhaps sometimes we don't need more faith—we just need more knowledge of whom we have faith in.

- *I have tried so hard and so often to change, but my problems are just too big for me to handle. Today I give up and throw myself totally on Your love and mercy.*

I felt this keenly during my Florida experience—and also during many other times in my life. No one is immune to problems, and if we're honest with ourselves, we'll recognize that we get in a good number of jams through our own choices.

The Bible often uses the metaphor of sheep to help explain human behavior and tendencies.

Sheep can be stubborn—just like humans. The neediest of all animals, sheep require constant care. There's even a term to describe one that ends up on its back, can't right itself, and kicks its feet in the air in panic—a "cast sheep." Fortunately, a shepherd can find a cast sheep, calm it down, and help it get back on its feet.

Just as a shepherd looks after a flock of sheep, our spiritual Father treats us with compassion and care—drawing near to us in tenderness and helping us cope with the difficulties and predicaments that confront us.

- *Cleanse me and change me from the inside out. Teach me how to imitate You, to have Your heart of kindness and mercy. Teach me to walk in the Spirit every day so I can know Your power and victory.*

When we become fully aware of how we're created and designed, we'll see that if we want to make relatively minor changes in our lives, it may be enough to focus on our basic attitudes and behaviors. However, if we want to make major changes, we need to review our paradigms and the way we view ourselves and the universe around us. We could call this sanctification.

In conclusion

It can be productive and insightful to ask these three questions of ourselves:

- *What would I do if I could not fail?*
- *Why not my best?*
- *What's really important in my life?*

Questions like these can give us clarity about the purpose of our lives. When we are called from the inside and pulled from above, that's when abundance abounds. The call is a summons from God to us personally and to live for His glory.

A surprising thing happens we're pulled upward and out of the various fears, discontentment and insecurities of life and into something which gives more meaning and purpose to all the complications and demands of our daily routines. We discover that we increasingly desire the understanding, compassion and love of Jesus.

We also understand that Satan tempts us in order to bring out the worst in us. This traps us in sin, guilt and fear. At the same time, God is testing our trust to bring out the best in our character and strengthen our faith. The battle is on for our mind. It's vital to understand this in order to make sense of our human condition and our present struggles in this environment. There are two distinct life forces in us, and they compete to control our thoughts, attitudes and behaviors. When we understand this, we're in a better situation to take advantage of the upward energy that's available to us.

CONCLUSION

Part I | *Taking action*

Congratulations on finishing the book. I hope you enjoy a small hit of dopamine for the accomplishment.

The basketball coach John Wooden once said, "Five years from now, you're the same person except for the people you've met and the books you've read." The experience of reading this book, I trust, will enrich your life in that sense—and supply you with all the power, balance and energy that you need to live a flourishing, beautiful and abundant life.

It's great that you read this book, but reading is just the first step. Please go back and study the concepts of power, balance and energy. That's what it will take for the Triangle Effect to become second nature to you and transform your life. I see people all the time who are busy enough but lack any real sense of direction or purpose. It seems like they're amateur actors on the stage, performing a role that they don't really own or inhabit.

My hope in writing this book was that I'd be able to equip readers with the tools, keys and solution strategies they need to think more deeply about their life's purpose and then to proactively move forward.

Think about that word *proactively*. If it didn't have *act* embedded right in the center of it, what would be the point of using it?

Action is a key concept of this book. Let's reflect on that for a moment.

Choice can be our greatest asset or our greatest liability—depending on what actions we decide to take. It's time to choose. If we don't choose now, then when? What is our unpainted canvas? Unwritten book? How is our life story going to play out? What's that one good habit we'd like to form and the one bad habit we'd like to break?  What dream is collecting dust on the shelf? What God-ordained passion is lying dormant in our lives?

Remember that we never finish what we don't start. Sometimes in life, it's easy for our routines to stymie our sense of adventure. We tend to play defense instead of offense. Our fears—rather than our hopes and dreams—dictate our decisions.

I appreciate what Leonardo da Vinci said along these lines: "Iron rusts from disuse; water loses its purity from stagnation...even so does inaction sap the vigor of the mind."

Reading this book won't do anyone any good unless it's followed by action. Here's an action step that I'd suggest. Write three positive and meaningful things on a 3x5 card and read them three times a day—morning, noon and night. Try that for three days, and you'll be amazed. Now take three cards and write three positive and meaningful things on each one, and read them all three times a day for three weeks—and you'll be changed. Now do the same for three months, and you'll be transformed.

Part II | *Thirty-three things*

Who doesn't like a good list? Information presented in this format can be accessible and actionable.

Here's my list of 33 things I've found to be very helpful in developing the power, balance and energy that we've spent this entire book unpacking.

1. *Listen.* We have two ears and only one mouth for a reason. Listen empathically.
2. *Study, learn and grow.* We're all stars—we just need to learn how to shine more.
3. *Be grateful.* We should express our gratitude anywhere, anytime and to anyone.
4. *Make and keep small commitments to others as well as to ourselves.* This creates momentum and patterns of positive energy.
5. *Get enough sleep.* We need at least seven to eight hours every night. Science tells us that the brain grows new connections during sleep. Adequate sleep gives us more emotional, mental and spiritual power.
6. *Spend time outside.* A long walk creates space for reflection and contemplation.
7. *Be a kind person in all situations.* This makes us healthier and happier, and it's contagious.
8. *Believe in miracles.* They happen every day!
9. *Use the power of choice wisely.* We all have the freedom to choose our response to any situation.
10. *Drink three large bottles of water daily.* This helps our body, mind and spirit.
11. *Be aware of the battle within.* The greatest battle we all face in our lives is the battle between our self-nature and our spiritual nature.

12. *An ounce of prevention is worth a pound of cure.* We need to think ahead and anticipate possible future regrets.

13. *Smile.* It improves our appearance and our attitude.

14. *Declutter.* This helps keep not only our spaces clear but also our mind.

15. *Laugh at the world.* There's a lot of material to work with, it's true—but this helps us not take ourselves too seriously.

16. *Don't worry.* Anxiety splits our energy between today's priorities and tomorrow's problems. Part of our mind is on the now, while the rest is on the "not yet." The result is half-minded living.

17. *Give in secret, with no thought of return.* And be generous even if we don't have much to give—with small acts of kindness, if nothing else.

18. *Carefully research investment tips.* An investment tip can be a dicey proposition and always requires due diligence. Remember, tips are for waiters, waitresses and bellhops.

19. *Live with enthusiasm.* It's like rocket fuel propelling achievement, and it's infectious.

20. *Don't ever quit.* Do you remember Herman Osgood? Neither does anyone else. He quit.

21. *Dream big.* Nothing big can be accomplished without a big dream.

22. *Understand essentialism.* Do less—but do it better.

23. *Stop.* To be more specific, stop playing the victim card, making excuses, letting the culture tell you how to live, trying to make other people happy, and doubting yourself.

24. *Focus on the right things.* In real estate, it's all about location, location, location. In investing, it's diversify, diversify, diversify. In life, it's trust, trust, trust.

25. *Connect with people.* We want to surround ourselves with the dreamers, the doers, the believers, the thinkers, and those who see the greatness within us. To have friends, be a friend.

26. *Plan your funeral*...at least in this sense: What do we want people to say about us at our funeral? Make a list, and live accordingly.
27. *Tend to your life's roots.* You can't have good fruit without good roots that reach down into rich soil.
28. *If you can't get out of a situation, get into it.* Embrace and learn from it.
29. *Write a letter to your future self every so often.* This aids in understanding life's trajectory.
30. *Focus on your purpose.* And realize that the purpose of your life is far greater than your own personal fulfillment and happiness.
31. *Save for a rainy day.* It's always better to have resources and not need them than to need resources and not have them.
32. *Deal with the difficult while it's easy.* Solve large problems while they're still small.
33. *Read the Bible from cover to cover.* It has a very happy ending.

Part III | *Final thoughts*

Looking back on the journey we've taken together, I'd describe part one—Power—as being about the 3 Gs: *grit* and the science of achievement, *gratitude* and the art of fulfillment, and *goals* with their inherent purpose and vision. These factors can make exciting things happen in our lives. We reviewed how real power is what we need in order to have an extraordinary, magnificent and abundant life.

Part two of the book, focusing on Balance, walked through the principles of maintaining a positive and productive equilibrium in the physical, mental and financial aspects of life.

And in part three, on Energy, we explored how we can be animated and motivated by inward, outward and upward energy. That latter kind of energy, whose source is God, is particularly important as it provides context and meaning for everything else in this book and in our lives.

Now that you've read about the Triangle Effect, I hope you'll understand that we are not victims of our circumstances, environment or biology—and that choices change our brain. If we change our perceptions, we can change and transform our lives. In a sense, our perceptions comprise our reality. The choices we make affect the wiring of our brain. How we understand and perceive our inner Spirit has a huge impact and transforms our lives. We can choose as an act of will to claim God as our life, power and identity.

This is not a self-help book because I've learned from experience (too many times) that strengthening the self can lead to a preoccupation with self—and that paradoxically brings about further self-imposed stress. To have absolute freedom, we need an absolute truth source. The Bible works for me.

Contrast that insight with the $20 billion self-help industry. The movement toward self-actualization, positive psychology and self-righteousness has major downsides and isn't sustainable. It all reminds me of the cheap appliances that are typically sold today. They have built-in, planned obsolescence. When they break down, it can be more cost-effective to just buy a new one.

Self-help approaches are not effective at creating lasting change. Why do I say that? There are three reasons:

- *They are not connected to the vine. They have no absolute truth source. They teach successful living without the author of the universe—Creator God—at the center and in full control.*

- *Their advice has lots of affirmations, visualizations and verbalizations, but the true intent of the heart is not considered. This creates cognitive dissonance or a disconnect between what's being said and what we really believe deep down in our innermost being. Without the Spirit, we would be just body and mind—leaving us bereft of power, balance and energy.*

- *These approaches don't leverage the spiritual or scientific principles that are required for meaningful change to take place. God tells us that because of free will, we have choices about how we focus our time, energy and attention.*

Now I want to leave readers with a personal note that points us all toward Almighty God. I believe that God looks at all of us with eyes of love. He knows our every need. He hears our heart's cry and wants us to reach out to Him. He desires for us to have blessings, happiness and joy in abundance.

When we see God for who He really is, we are utterly and completely transformed. The Holy Spirit does not come into our lives to patch up our current identity but to give us a new identity as a redeemed child of God. No longer do we identify as inferior, insecure and inadequate. All of that baggage is exchanged for a new identity in Christ. Now we have the peace that surpasses all understanding.

I hope that the journey we've taken in this book leads all readers to the *incomparable* journey that awaits—in communion with God our Creator, Redeemer and Friend.

THREE 3X5 CARDS FOR THE ROAD

"Don't copy the behavior and customs of this world, but let God transform you into a new person by changing the way you think. Then you will learn to know God's will for you, which is good and pleasing and perfect."—*Romans 12:2 (NLT)*

"We can rejoice, too, when we run into problems and trials, for we know that they help us develop endurance. And endurance develops strength of character, and character strengthens our confident hope of salvation. And this hope will not lead to disappointment. For we know how dearly God loves us, because he has given us the Holy Spirit to fill our hearts with his love."— *Romans 5:3-5 (NLT)*

"They replied, 'We want to perform God's works, too. What should we do?' Jesus told them, 'This is the only work God wants from you: Believe in the one he has sent.'"—*John 6:28-29 (NLT)*

MCKENNA, CLARK, MAXTON AND HOGAN

I hope you realize how much I love you guys.

Now maybe you'll understand your Pop-Pop better—
and why I love my 3x5 card collection so much!

APPENDIX A

List of personal values:

1. authenticity	21. kindness
2. adventure	22. knowledge
3. balance	23. leadership
4. bravery	24. learning
5. compassion	25. love
6. challenge	26. loyalty
7. citizenship	27. openness
8. community	28. optimism
9. creativity	29. recognition
10. curiosity	30. respect
11. determination	31. responsibility
12. fairness	32. security
13. freedom	33. self-respect
14. friendships	34. social connection
15. fun	35. spirituality
16. generosity	36. stability
17. growth	37. status
18. honesty	38. wealth
19. integrity	39. wisdom
20. justice	

—https://www.psychologytoday.com/us/blog/click-here-happiness/201807/39-core-values-and- how-live-them

APPENDIX B

What do you want? What is most important?
Payoffs that people often seek from their work.

The list below consists of 17 possible reasons that people have for working. Each word or phrase can be used to answer the question, "What do I want to get out of the effort I'm putting into my work?"

Knowledge: To pursue and learn about new things and ideas; to search for truth, or information; to be known by others as an intelligent person and feel intelligent.

Power: To lead and direct others; to influence or control others, i.e., to get them to do what I want them to do.

Independence: To achieve my own goals in the manner best suited to me; to have freedom to come and go as I wish; to be myself at all times; to control my own actions.

Accomplishments: To achieve my personal objectives with a sense that I've done something as well as, if not better than, someone else; to experience self-satisfaction when I rise to a challenge, accomplish a task or a job, or solve a problem.

Recognition: To receive attention, notice, approval, or respect from others because of something I've done; to generate a feeling in others for who I am and what I achieve.

Friendship: To have many friends; to work with others and enjoy their camaraderie; to join groups for companionship; to look forward to and enjoy social relations.

Responsibility: To be held accountable to others or to organizations to which I belong for a job or task; to possess something and care for it.

Creativity: To have the ability, desire, and freedom to develop new ideas, solutions to problems, improvements in products or procedures, or designs of things or plans; to be mentally challenged; to be first to innovate or create.

Security: To possess the basic wherewithal for living; to feel safe; to have self-confidence; to have job security and continuity of income.

Dedication: To be loyal to the company or my supervisor, my family, social and political groups, and others; to give devotion, commitment, or friendship to others.

Justice and parity: To receive rewards and recognition for my contributions and achievements in proportion to my effort and comparable with those received by other people.

Growth: To advance, to expand my life through my job and through the improvement of my status at work or in the community; to increase my work- and nonwork-related knowledge or skills; to find fulfillment in the groups in which I work or live; to mature personally and professionally.

Self-esteem: To be someone of value in my own and other people's eyes: to be accepted as a person instead of a nonentity or a means to an end; to feel useful and wanted by other people; to be a leader; to be appreciated by others.

Challenge: To feel good about what I do, its degree of difficult, and the complexity or demands on my creativity; to have opportunities to apply my knowledge and skills effectively and easily.

Helpfulness: To provide assistance, support, empathy, or protection to others: to be open, responsive, and generous.

Money: To have sufficient income or other assets to use as I wish; to be materially comfortable or well off.

Good times/pleasure: To have fun; to enjoy myself; to do the things I like to do instead of only the things I have to do.

—*Source unknown*

Printed in the United States
by Baker & Taylor Publisher Services